INDUS ENIGMA

Indus Enigma

CHRONICLES OF A SILENT CIVILIZATION

MACK RAFEAL

Spectra Enterprise

Contents

INDEX

5.3 Delve into the moral dilemma of revealing the truth versus preserving secrets

5.4 A journey through remote locations, ancient caves, and forgotten temples

Chapter 6: Timeless Connections

6.1 The protagonist uncovers links between the ancient civilization and present-day cultures

6.2 Flashbacks to historical events that might have influenced the Indus Valley Civilization

6.3 Unravel the connection between the lost language and modern languages

6.4 Discovery of a hidden chamber with artifacts hinting at advanced technology

Chapter 7: Unveiling the Enigma

7.1 Climax: Confrontation with the secret society and decoding the final piece of the puzzle

7.2 Revelation of the civilization's purpose and the reason behind its disappearance

7.3 Reflection on the implications of the discovered knowledge on modern society

7.4 Closing scenes with the protagonist sharing the truth with the world and the legacy of the Indus Valley Civilization

INTRODUCTION

A gripping voyage into the mysteries of the ancient Indus Valley Civilization, "Indus Enigma: Chronicles of a Silent Civilization" combines aspects of archeology, linguistics, and speculative fiction to create a compelling narrative. The story is told from the perspective of a dogged archaeologist who is determined to uncover the long-lost secrets of a civilization that has been lost to the sands of time. The setting of the story is the lonely ruins of Mohenjo-Daro and Harappa.

The Story in Brief:

A series of mysterious objects, which are dispersed fragments that defy conventional explanation, are found at the beginning of the novel. This discovery prompts the protagonist to start on a journey to find answers to the questions asked. As the archaeologist continues to investigate the ruins, the reverberations of the once-thriving civilization begin to become audible. These echoes hint at a language that has been lost and a story that has not been told yet and is waiting to be discovered.

Together, the protagonist and the genius linguist travel the linguistic labyrinth that is etched into the very fabric of the ancient city. This is done in the pursuit of deciphering the enigmatic symbols that have been left behind. The quest turns into a race against time and a battle against the weather as the two individuals attempt to understand inscriptions that offer glimpses into the everyday lives, governance, and spiritual traditions of the mysterious civilization.

The protagonist is forced to confront not just the historical narrative but also a covert organization known as the Guardians of the Past as a result of discoveries made in hidden chambers that show scrolls that have been maintained in good condition. This covert organization emerges as a strong foe, intent on safeguarding the secrets of civilization and preventing the disclosure of a truth that has the potential to transform our view of the sequence of events that have occurred throughout human history.

"Indus Enigma" examines the moral conundrums that the protagonist must face as the story progresses. These include the ethical consequences of exposing ancient information as opposed to the preservation of historical mysteries. The voyage brings the archaeologist closer to discovering the truth and deeper into the shadows of history with each step that he makes. The adventure takes unexpected twists via distant locales, ancient caves, and lost temples.

An encounter with the Guardians of the Past serves as the climactic conflict. It is during this encounter that the protagonist is able to decode the final piece of the puzzle, which exposes the purpose of the civilization as well as the reasons surrounding its departure. The revelation is not just a victory of archaeological discovery, but it is also a confrontation with the legacy of the Indus Valley Civilization and the ramifications that it has for both the present and the future.

The development of characters:

By the end of the story, the protagonist has developed into a multifaceted figure who is motivated by an unquenchable thirst for knowledge and an unrelenting determination to discover the truth. Both intellectually and emotionally, a tremendous transformation takes place as a result of the difficulties encountered in deciphering the old language and navigating the treacherous trip.

Additional characters, such as the linguistic expert and members of the Guardians of the Past, contribute to the narrative's depth and complexity by providing additional layers of information. Every single character contributes their own distinct point of view, set of goals, and conflicts to the table, which all contribute to the intricate tapestry that is the plot.

Various Themes:

The film "Indus Enigma" delves into a wide range of topics, such as the unrelenting quest for information, the repercussions of unearthing long-lost mysteries, the moral obligations of people who possess historical truths, and the enduring linkages that exist between ancient civilizations and modern-day societies. The narrative dives into the human preoccupation with the unknown, the precarious nature of historical legacies, and the influence that historical revelations have on the society of today.

Notable Implications and Contemplations:

Beyond its fictitious plot, "Indus Enigma" is significant for a number of other reasons as well. It encourages readers to contemplate the gaps in our knowledge of past civilizations as well as the potential repercussions that could result from discovering information about such civilizations. As a mirror to our own curiosity-driven endeavors and the ethical issues that are inherent in the pursuit of knowledge, the discovery of linguistic problems, archeological wonders, and moral quandaries acts as a mirror.

In the last chapters, the protagonist reveals the newly discovered information to the rest of the world, and the narrative evolves into a contemplation on the significance of history in the formation of collective identity, as well as the obligations that come with having insights into the past.

The legacy of the civilization that flourished in the Indus Valley becomes a metaphor for the tenacity of human curiosity and the significant influence that historical revelations have had on the course of human history.

It is through the weaving together of aspects of mystery, adventure, and historical exploration that "Indus Enigma: Chronicles of a Silent Civilization" is able to construct a narrative that transcends time and captivates the imagination. The work invites readers to embark on a voyage of discovery by means of its sophisticated plot, well-developed characters, and examination of significant issues. This trip is a reflection of the same quest for understanding that is the essence of the human spirit. As the mystery surrounding the civilization of the Indus Valley is revealed, the story leaves a lasting impact on the reader, prompting them to examine the connectivity of the past, the present, and the future.

Chapter 1

Unveiling Shadows

In the realms of literature, art, philosophy, and even in day-to-day life, the metaphorical concept of "Unveiling Shadows" bears a great deal of significance. This theme goes beyond its literal interpretation, diving into the realms of discovery, enlightenment, and the unveiling of truths that have been concealed. "Unveiling Shadows" encourages us to investigate the mysteries that are hidden under the surface, from the shadows that linger in the corners of our brains to the metaphorical darkness that obscures historical narratives. This calls us to investigate the mysteries that lie beneath the surface.

In the realm of literature, shadows:

The shadows that appear in works of literature frequently function as metaphors for the unknown, the repressed, or the features of characters and plotlines that are hidden from view. The shadows of characters can be seen as a representation of their concealed motivations, inner conflicts, or the more negative aspects of their personality. Novels such as "Heart of Darkness" by Joseph Conrad and "Strange Case of Dr. Jekyll and Mr. Hyde" by Robert Louis Stevenson are examples of how shadows are used in literature to depict the complexities of human nature.

An analogy can be drawn between the process of uncovering shadows in literature and the voyage of self-discovery and the finding of truths that have been buried. There is a possibility that characters will struggle with their own shadows, confronting their own inner demons and going through the murky depths of their mind. It is the revelation of shadows that becomes a critical point as the story progresses. This moment propels the plot ahead and provides readers with important insights into the human condition.

The Role of Shadows in Art:

Shadows are exceptionally important in the field of visual arts because they contribute to the creation of depth, contrast, and atmosphere. The manipulation of shadows by artists is a skillful technique that allows them to create feelings, highlight key points, and endow their works with multiple layers of meaning. When light and shadow interact with one another, it becomes a metaphor for the way in which knowledge and ignorance, clarity and obscurity, interact with one another.

Take, for example, the chiaroscuro method that was utilized by artists such as Caravaggio, Rembrandt, and Leonardo da Vinci. Not only were these masters able to create visually magnificent compositions by utilizing the dramatic interplay of light and shadow, but they also utilized shadows as a symbol to represent the complexity and nuances of the human experience. "Unveiling Shadows" in art becomes a process of unveiling layers of significance, enabling spectators to explore the hidden narratives that are contained inside the artwork.

The shadows in philosophical thought:

The idea of shadows has been investigated from a philosophical standpoint in a number of different traditions. For example, in Plato's Allegory of the Cave, there is a powerful metaphor in which people who are locked up inside a cave can only see shadows thrown on the wall by things that are behind them. Breaking away from these shadows and advancing to the realm of genuine knowledge are both necessary steps on the path to enlightenment.

The concept of "unveiling shadows" in philosophy goes beyond the physical act of seeing and encompasses the metaphorical unveiling of truths that have been shrouded by ignorance or delusion over the course of human history. In doing so, it speaks to the human yearning for insight and wisdom, as well as the realization that our views are frequently colored by the shadows of our own prejudices.

When it comes to psychology, shadows:

Shadows take on a psychological significance within the field of psychology, where they are interpreted as symbolizing the components of the mind that are not conscious. The "shadow self" is a concept that was developed by Carl Jung. It dives into the aspects of an individual's personality that are concealed and frequently suppressed. Being confronted with and integrating these shadow qualities is an essential part of the process of self-discovery, which ultimately results in personal development and a more genuine living.

In the field of psychology, "Unveiling Shadows" is transformed into a therapeutic journey, a process that involves bringing the concealedness into conscious awareness. In order to achieve a more holistic and integrated sense of self, it is necessary to recognize and accept aspects of oneself that may have been hidden from view in the past.

There are shadows in history:

Shadows cast by time can obscure or distort our perception of the past when it comes to the background of history. There is a high probability that historical accounts contain elements of prejudice, omission, or misrepresentation. For the purpose of "Unveiling Shadows" in history, it is necessary to do a thorough investigation of original materials, to conduct an analysis of views, and to make a commitment to exposing voices that have been hidden or ignored.

The study of history transforms into an ongoing process that involves revealing things that were previously hidden, bringing to light stories that have not been told, and contesting the dominant narratives. This can be seen in movements that are attempting to examine historical accounts from a variety of perspectives, so addressing the shadows that have hidden the realities of oppressed people.

In the process of personal development, revealing shadows:

On a more personal level, the concept of "Unveiling Shadows" is an essential component in the process of coming into one's own and developing as a person. Every single person harbors inside them characteristics that may be concealed from their conscious consciousness, such as worries, insecurities, and previous traumatic experiences. Introspection, vulnerability, and a willingness to confront the intricacies of one's own psyche are all necessary components of the process of revealing these shadows.

Individuals have the opportunity to reveal their shadows through the use of therapeutic approaches such as psychoanalysis, mindfulness, and expressive arts. The objective is not just to confront the more negative parts, but also to incorporate them into a self-narrative that is more consistent and genuine. Individuals are able to cultivate resilience, self-compassion, and a greater awareness of their own narratives through the process of revealing their personal shadows, which becomes a transformative process.

The Revealing of Hidden Facets Found in Technology:

When applied to the sphere of technology, the metaphor of shadows takes on new dimensions in this age of digitized technology. Questions regarding transparency, accountability, and the ethical consequences of technological breakthroughs are raised as a result of the shadows cast by algorithms, issues regarding data privacy, and the digital footprint that each human leaves behind.

Not only does the unveiling of shadows in technology require a grasp of the algorithms that form our experiences online, but it also requires a grappling with the broader societal effects of a digital landscape that is continually expanding. A nuanced investigation into the shadows that are thrown by the incorporation of technology into every aspect of our life is required because of this occurrence.

Within the realms of literature, art, philosophy, psychology, history, human development, and technology, "Unveiling Shadows" emerges as a theme that is both diverse and abundant in its pervasiveness. It extends an invitation to us to confront the veiled parts of existence, whether they are found within ourselves, in the narratives of the past, or in the environment of the present, which is constantly changing.

To embark on journeys of discovery, enlightenment, and transformation, we must first uncover the shadows that we have been hiding. The concept of "Unveiling

Shadows" resonates as a universal and eternal motif that speaks to the essence of the human experience. This is true whether it is explored through the artistic portrayal of light and dark on a canvas, the philosophical discovery of hidden truths, or the personal quest for self-understanding.

1.1 Introduction to the mysterious Indus Valley Civilization

The Indus Valley Civilization, which is considered to be one of the oldest and most mysterious civilizations in the world, flourished in the broad plains of the Indus River, which are located in what is now Pakistan and northwest India. The Harappan Civilization, which was called after the ancient city of Harappa, lived from around 3300 BCE to 1300 BCE and were the predecessors to both the Egyptian and Mesopotamian civilizations. It is commonly referred to as the Harappan Civilization. In spite of the fact that it made enormous contributions to the history of humanity, the Indus Valley Civilization continues to be cloaked in mystery. Numerous features of its culture, language, and fall continue to defy decisive explanation.

Geographical Location:

The Indus Valley Civilization was established in a location that possessed a rich and fertile landscape, which encompassed the floodplains of the Indus River and its tributaries. This led to the establishment of the basis for civilization. Due to the fact that the river provided nourishment through its annual floods, the geographical setting had a significant role in the flourishing of civilization. This was because the river made agricultural practices easier to implement, which in turn supported a more populous populace.

The towns of the Indus Valley, such as Mohenjo-Daro and Harappa, were established in such a way that they were strategically positioned along the riverbanks. These cities displayed superior urban planning by having well-laid-out roadways, sophisticated drainage systems, and the construction of multistory brick constructions. It is possible that these cities were organized with such thorough attention to detail that they exhibited a level of central authority and municipal planning that was unmatched at that era.

Advancing the Case for Urban Planning:

It is the superior urban planning that is the defining characteristic of the Indus Valley Civilization. This civilization was distinguished by cities that were precisely constructed and showed a high degree of social organization. The streets were organized in a grid form, and the buildings were built using bricks that were produced according to a standard. It is noteworthy that the cities demonstrated a wonderful mastery of urban sanitation. They included an intricate drainage system that included covered sewers beneath the streets, which offered a glimpse into their civic engineering expertise.

The Great Bath, which is a massive water tank that was discovered in Mohenjo-Daro, is yet another example of the advanced urban planning that the civilization accomplished. Questions are raised on the social and religious significance of water in their society as a result of this well-engineered edifice that was erected with precision and care.

Activities Related to the Economy:

Agriculture and trade were the bedrock upon which the economic basis of the Indus Valley Civilization was constructed. The river valley's rich soil made it possible to cultivate a wide range of crops, including wheat, barley, and cotton, among others because of its favorable conditions. Archaeological evidence points to the existence of a highly developed agricultural system that made extensive use of irrigation in order to achieve maximum productivity.

Artifacts found at excavation sites demonstrate that the civilization had a network of trading channels that extended to Mesopotamia and other regions. This indicates that trade played a significant role in the economic activities of the civilization. An exquisite carving of animals can be seen on the seals that were discovered in the ruins. This suggests that there was a script or symbolism system that has not been decoded.

A Mysterious Writing System:

The written script of the Indus Valley Civilization is one of the most intriguing mysteries that surrounds this mysterious civilization. Linguists and archaeologists have been confounded for decades by the fact that the Harappan writing, which was found on seals, pottery, and other artifacts, has not been deciphered for the time being. There is no Rosetta Stone counterpart that has been discovered to provide a key to the translation of the script, despite the fact that the script is composed of a collection of symbols and characters.

The lack of documents that have been decoded makes it difficult for us to comprehend the written works of the civilization, as well as its administrative structures and even its spoken language. Our understanding of the intellectual and communication accomplishments of the Harappan culture is significantly lacking due to the fact that the linguistic code of the Harappan script continues to be a mystery, despite the various attempts that have been completed.

Symbolism and Artifacts of Cultural Significance:

It is possible to gain insights into the Indus Valley Civilization's art, craftsmanship, and societal ideals through the material culture of the civilization, which is abundant and full of variety. Their artistic abilities are demonstrated by the fact that they discovered intricate pieces of jewelry, pottery, and sculptures. Among the most notable items are the well-known figurine of a dancing girl and the Pashupati seal, which depicts a deity in a yoga position.

The fact that particular symbols, such as the unicorn or the bull, are frequently used in their artwork provides evidence that they used a symbolic language to communicate cultural, religious, or societal values. On the other hand, the true significance of these symbols is still unknown, which contributes to the general mystique that surrounds the civilization when taken into consideration.

Religion and Social Organization:

The social structure of the civilization that flourished in the Indus Valley is still a topic of investigation among academics. As a result of the absence of massive structures that are normally associated with palaces or temples, discussions have arisen over the nature of religious rituals and the administrative system. Questions regarding the political and social organization of the civilization are raised by the egalitarian layout of cities and the absence of apparent signs of social hierarchy amongst the various social groups.

There is also the mystery surrounding the religion that existed within the Indus Valley Civilization. The absence of monumental religious structures raises doubts regarding the nature of their worship and spiritual activities, despite the fact that the finding of seals showing probable deities shows that their society may have a religious component.

A decline and disappearance of the species:

It is possible that the most obscure parts of the history of the Indus Valley Civilization are the decline and eventual disappearance of that civilization. There was a gradual departure of urban centers, which marked the beginning of the decline of the cities about the year 1900 BCE. Environmental variables such as climate change, floods, or variations in river flows are among the hypotheses that have been presented to explain this reduction. Other hypotheses include potential socio-political upheavals. The reasons for this decline are still a matter of speculation.

Academics have been forced to explore internal factors, such as the depletion of resources or societal discontent, as plausible contributors to the fall because there is no clear evidence of violent invasions or conquests. An important turning point in human history occurred when the once-thriving urban centers of the Indus Valley Civilization were gradually reclaimed by nature. This event, regardless of the cause, marks a critical milestone in human history.

Legacy and Influence:

In spite of the fact that the Indus Valley Civilization existed for only a short period of time and was shrouded in mystery, its legacy continues to live on in a variety of ways. Historical precedents were established for subsequent societies in the Indian subcontinent as a result of the advanced urban planning, engineering marvels, and agricultural methods that were displayed by the civilization.

The vestiges of the Harappan writing and symbols continue to be present in the cultural fabric of the region, serving as a source of inspiration for contemporary art and design.

To add insult to injury, the mystery surrounding the civilization that flourished in the Indus Valley continues to captivate the imaginations of archaeologists, academics, and fans alike. The ongoing excavations and developments in archaeological techniques hold the possibility of revealing other riddles, which will result in a more profound comprehension of this ancient society and the contributions it made to the history of humanity.

One of the most impressive examples of the inventiveness and tenacity of ancient human societies is the civilization that flourished in the Indus Valley. The attraction that surrounds this ancient society is a result of the advanced urban planning, clever engineering, and mysterious script that it possesses. We are invited to embark on a trip of investigation by the enigma of the Indus Valley Civilization. This adventure will allow us to dig into the shadows of the past and uncover the secrets that continue to evade our comprehension. In spite of the fact that continuing study and excavations are shedding new light on this ancient civilization, the legacy of the Indus Valley continues to be a riveting chapter in the annals of human history. It invites us to uncover the secrets that linger in its silent ruins.

1.2 Discovery of ancient artifacts, triggering intrigue and curiosity

One of the reasons why history is so fascinating is that it has the power to take us back in time, giving us a glimpse of the lives and cultures that existed before our own. The unearthing of ancient artifacts works as a portal to the past, providing a concrete link to the narratives that have played a significant role in the development of humanity. This study into the uncovering of relics, each of which has its own story to tell, arouses an innate interest, which in turn sparks a trip into the depths of antiquity.

The Fascinating Introductory Plot:

The story starts off with a serendipitous event, which is the accidental discovery made by an archaeologist that makes a significant change in the way historical knowledge developed. The unearthing of long-lost relics in a dusty museum base-ment or the excavation of an unexplored archeological site are two examples of how the discovery of ancient items frequently begins as an exciting prelude to a more extensive narrative.

Consider the following scenario: a group of archaeologists are painstakingly working their way through the layers of dirt, their equipment rubbing against the relics of an old civilization. Unexpectedly, the gleam of metal or the trace of an elaborate carving that has been concealed for generations beneath the embrace of the soil has become visible.

First and foremost, this finding lays the groundwork for a journey that will involve unraveling mysteries and gaining insight into the lives of those who came before.

An Archaeological Expedition:

The process of unearthing ancient artifacts is not a straightforward endeavor; rather, it comprises an archaeological expedition that is meticulously planned and carried out. When it comes to exposing the past, researchers and professionals gather at locations that hold historical value, armed with shovels, brushes, and an uncompromising zeal for doing so. In the process of selecting excavation sites, historical records, satellite photography, and even a little bit of intuition are frequently used as sources of information.

In and of itself, the excavation process is a delicate ballet that requires both patience and concentration. Through the process of peeling away each layer of earth, a different chapter in the history of the location is revealed. Fragments of pottery, tools, jewelry, and pieces of once-grand structures are beginning to appear, each piece adding to the mosaic of the past that is being created. The excitement of discovery is amplified with each relic that is uncovered, as archaeologists meticulously document their discoveries and theorize about the civilization that once flourished in that same location.

The artifact as a time capsule

There is more to an ancient relic than just a thing; it is a time capsule that captures the essence of the age in which it was created. Taking into consideration a figurine that has been finely carved, the craftsmanship not only represents the abilities of the artisan who created it, but it also reflects the aesthetic preferences and cultural values of the society that produced it. The fragment of pottery, which is adorned with symbols that have faded with time, transforms into a linguistic puzzle, providing tantalizing glimpses into the language that was spoken by the people who created it.

This collection of artifacts serves as silent witnesses to the rituals, technologies, and daily lives of civilizations that have long since passed away. In light of the fact that modern technology enables researchers to apply methods like carbon dating, CT scans, and 3D modeling to extract even more information from the artifacts without causing any damage to them, it is imperative that these treasures be meticulously preserved.

Concerning the Initiation of Curiosity and Intrigue:

Discovering ancient artifacts is inextricably tied to the human propensity for curiosity and the desire to solve the secrets of the past. This is because humans have a natural fascination with the past. The artifacts in question are not merely relics; rather, they are clues in an old detective story that invite us to piece together the story of those who came before us.

The mysteries are not only contained inside the relics themselves, but also within the questions that they raise and the tales that they hold back from being revealed.

All people are drawn to these artifacts for their appeal. When ancient objects are discovered, they arouse an intense curiosity in people of all ages and backgrounds, from seasoned archaeologists to casual history enthusiasts. This curiosity is a search for understanding that goes beyond the confines of time. The objects encourage us to reflect on the lives of ancient peoples, including their achievements and their challenges, as well as the cultural tapestry that has been created over the time period.

Cultural Significance:

In addition to the domains of history and archaeology, the discovery of ancient objects carries with it a significant cultural weight. These relics are not only relics from a bygone era; rather, they represent concrete connections to the cultural history and identity of the people who own them. It is through museums that the public is given the opportunity to identify with their roots and to appreciate the diversity of human civilization. Museums become the stewards of these riches.

Consider, for example, the discovery of relics from an ancient market square, which consisted of a mosaic of tools, currencies, and items that were associated with trading. It is not only the discovery that offers information on economic behaviors, but it also illustrates the interconnectivity of ancient communities. These kinds of discoveries arouse curiosity not only about the particular civilization that is being investigated, but also about the larger web of human contact and exchange.

Challenges and Controversies:

Discovering ancient treasures is a quest that is not without difficulties and debates along the way. There are further levels of complexity added to the story by the ethical problems that accompany excavation, the ownership of artifacts, and the possibility of looting archeological sites. The obligation of maintaining the cultural heritage of nations must be balanced with the pursuit of knowledge in order to achieve a desirable equilibrium.

The removal of artifacts from their country of origin and their subsequent placement in the collections of institutions located in other countries frequently gives rise to instances of controversy. This ongoing conversation concerning the ethics of archaeological procedures and the lawful ownership of historical objects is highlighted by the call for repatriation, which refers to the process of returning cultural treasures to the locations where they were originally discovered within the world.

Technological Developments in the Field of Exploration:

Discovering ancient artifacts has been substantially facilitated by technological advancements, which have made the procedure significantly longer. Archaeologists are able to quickly survey huge regions and discover possible sites for excavation by utilizing remote sensing techniques. Some examples of these techniques include ground-penetrating radar and LiDAR (Light Detection and Ranging). In order to uncover previously concealed archeological artifacts and constructions, drones that are fitted with high-resolution cameras are able to provide bird's-eye views of landscapes.

The use of scientific methods in the laboratory, including as DNA analysis, isotope investigations, and radiocarbon dating, provides insights into the origins, relationships, and chronology of ancient civilizations that have never been seen before. Not only do these technical tools make the excavation process more efficient, but they also help to a more in-depth comprehension of the artifacts and the communities that were responsible for their creation.

Bringing to Light the Hidden Faces of the Past:

When it comes down to it, the process of uncovering the shadows of the past is what the discovery of ancient artifacts is all about. Each item carries with it the echoes of a society that has long since vanished, and it invites us to determine the language of that civilization, understand its symbols, and reconstruct the stories that are inscribed within it. During the process of unearthing treasures from the depths of antiquity, we are simultaneously confronted with the shadows that veil the stories of those who came before us.

It is possible that the shadows will take the form of languages that have been lost, paints that have faded on pottery, or the shattered remnants of buildings that were once big and imposing. In order to uncover these shadows, a multidisciplinary approach is required, one that brings together the knowledge and experience of scientists, linguists, historians, and archaeologists. The reconstruction of the mosaic of human history is a collaborative effort that aims to breathe life into the shards that have been left behind.

There is no such thing as a finite undertaking when it comes to the discovery of ancient objects; rather, it is a continuum, a process of constant discovery and rediscovery. As new technologies come into existence, as archeological methods continue to advance, and as our comprehension of the past becomes more profound, the story of ancient civilizations continues to be told. Each new artifact that is unearthed adds a new chapter to the continuous narrative of humanity. It makes a contribution to our collective knowledge and reshapes our perceptions of the past.

The unearthing of ancient artifacts is a demonstration of the insatiable curiosity of humans and the pursuit of gaining an understanding of our origins. It is a trip into the shadows of the past, where each artifact becomes a beacon, lighting the narratives of civilizations that have long since passed away. By delving into the shards of history, we not only discover the answers to the mysteries of long-lost civilizations, but we also set out on an adventure that will last forever: an investigation into the human experience. In the past, the relics were silent; however, they now speak volumes, asking us to listen to the echoes of the past and learn from them.

1.3 Introduce the protagonist, an archaeologist eager to unravel the enigma

Our story begins with the introduction of a central individual, the protagonist, in the heart of the mysterious Indus Valley Civilization, where the echoes of an ancient civilization linger in the ruins of Mohenjo-Daro and Harappa. This is where our story begins to unfold. Archaeologist who is driven by an insatiable curiosity, an unbreakable passion for the past, and a tireless desire to solve the mystery that lays dormant in the silent ruins of history might be described as someone who is driven by these three things.

This is the Call of the Past:

Our main character, whose name may be inscribed in the annals of archeological investigation, is not only a scientist who is armed with tools and brushes; rather, he is a seeker of stories and a listener to the whispers of the past. Not in the sterile confines of a laboratory, but rather in the broad, sun-drenched plains where the relics of an ancient civilization are waiting to be discovered, they begin their trip away from the laboratory.

Ever since he was a child, the main character has had a strong connection to the relics leftover from the past. The protagonist's passion with the past was visible all throughout the novel, whether it was through their visits to the neighborhood museum, their reading of history books, or their participation in spontaneous archeological digs in their garden. The fascination of unearthing the stories that had been buried beneath layers of time became an irresistible force, and it began to shape their future at a young age.

Exceptional Academic Capabilities and Expertise:

Additionally, the protagonist's commitment to the pursuit of knowledge grows as they progress through the story. Their competence is built on a solid foundation of a superb academic record in archaeology and other subjects related to it. A scholar who is well-versed in archaeological techniques, historical settings, and the inter-disciplinary nature of their profession, the protagonist is not only an explorer who is venturing into the past; rather, they are a scholar who is armed with a profound understanding of these matters.

In order to achieve academic success, one must devote years to hard study, extensive fieldwork, and close collaboration with other researchers. As a result of the protagonist's significant contributions to the area, which included the discovery of previously unknown parts of ancient civilizations, the protagonist may have received notoriety. The combination of their extensive knowledge and unquench-able curiosity has propelled them to the forefront of an archaeological research movement.

Motivation on an Individual Level:

There is a personal motivation that drives the protagonist onward, which lies beneath the layers of professional dedication that comprise the protagonist. Maybe there is a family tradition about an ancestor who was related to an old civilization. This is a story that has been passed down from generation to generation, and it is this story that sparked the protagonist's interest. It's also possible that the spark of interest was kindled by an experience that occurred during childhood with an artifact, such as an heirloom that had a mystery history.

The personal connection that the protagonist has to the past serves as a driving factor, producing an emotional undercurrent that gives the protagonist's mission additional dimension. In addition to unearthing archeological facts, it is also about reclaiming stories that have been forgotten and establishing a connection with the human experiences that have been passed down through the ages.

The mystery surrounding the Indus Valley:

There is a magnetic attraction that pulls the protagonist into an adventure of a lifetime, and that force is the mystery surrounding the civilization that existed in the Indus Valley. The siren's call is the tempting signs of an advanced society, the undeciphered script, and the unresolved riddles of its decline. These elements become the siren's call, beckoning the archaeologist to journey into the heart of the ancient enigma.

The most difficult endeavor that the protagonist undertakes takes place in the Indus Valley, which is known for its deserted ruins and hidden mysteries. Their tenacity is fueled by the appeal of interpreting the script, comprehending the cultural complexities, and finding the solution to the mystery of the disappearance of civilization. The protagonist embarks on a voyage that goes beyond the confines of time for the purpose of solving the riddle, which transforms from merely an intellectual endeavor into a personal mission.

Obstacles in One's Personal and Professional Life:

The trip that the protagonist takes, however, is not devoid of obstacles.

The unpleasant realities of archeological investigation, such as digging in the sweltering heat of the sun, carefully sorting through layers of soil, and dealing with the unpredictability of funding and assistance, become essential components of their narrative. There are times of self-doubt, personal sacrifices, and strained relationships that are woven into the fabric of the narrative.

It is important to note that the protagonist's hardships are not confined to the realms of physical and professional challenges. There are times when the mysteries of the present are mirrored by the enigmas of the past, which can result in internal conflicts and ethical conundrums among individuals. As an archaeologist, you are tasked with the responsibility of unearthing the truth, striking a balance between your academic objectives and the demands of society, and confronting the shadows of history. All of these factors add to the overarching narrative of your journey.

Collaborations and Alliances:

The practice of archaeology is rarely a solitary activity. When the protagonist realizes the magnitude of the mystery they are attempting to solve, they begin to create alliances and collaborate with other characters. During the journey, the protagonist is accompanied by a wide group of specialists, including geologists, historians, and linguists. The multidimensional investigation of the ancient civilization is facilitated by the contributions of each individual member, who contributes their own set of abilities and points of view.

The narrative is made more complex by the tensions that exist within the team. A microcosm that is indicative of the greater archeological community is created via the victories of collaboration and the inevitable disputes that arise. In order for the protagonist to be successful in his mission to discover the secrets of the Indus

Valley, the relationships that are created and the expertise that is exchanged become vital components.

Deciphering the Language of the Past:

The deciphering of the mysterious script that is found on artifacts and structures all around the Indus Valley is an essential part of the mission that the protagonist is on. When the protagonist works together with linguists and language experts to decipher the coded signals from a civilization that has been lost in time, the linguistic challenge becomes the primary focus of the story.

One of the most important aspects of the archeological expedition is the meticulous attempts that are being made to crack the code. These efforts include comparing symbols, evaluating trends, and cross-referencing with other scripts that are known. The protagonist's intellectual fortitude and persistence in the face of historical ambiguity are mirrored in the successes and failures that occur in the process of understanding the language of the past throughout the story.

Considerations of an Ethical Nature:

During the course of the protagonist's journey through the various layers of history, ethical questions are brought to the forefront. There are a number of issues that weigh heavily on the protagonist's conscience, including the question of who owns artifacts, the influence that archeological activities have on the communities that are located nearby, and the obligation of uncovering historical truths.

By compelling the protagonist to confront not just the shadows of the past but also the ethical shadows that follow the pursuit of knowledge, the ethical difficulties provide moral complexity to the narrative and force the protagonist to confront both ethical and historical shadows. When it comes to the journey of an archaeologist, striking a balance between the need to be sensitive to different cultures and the drive to uncover the truth becomes an essential component.

Moments of Revelation:

There are moments of revelation that punctuate the tale here and there, despite the difficulties and ethical problems that are there. Whether it be the digging of a well-preserved item, the successful deciphering of a piece of the script, or the finding of a hidden chamber, all of these events become important moments that bring the protagonist closer to solving the mystery.

These moments of revelation are not merely intellectual achievements; rather, they are windows into the lives of the ancient society. A significant connection is made between the protagonist and the people who previously inhabited the silent ruins as the protagonist stands at the confluence of the past and the present. At the same time that the mysteries of the past are beginning to be revealed, the riddle is beginning to reveal its secrets.

The culmination of the protagonist's journey is not simply the revelation of historical truths; rather, it is a transformation—an evolution that is formed by the challenges, revelations, and ethical considerations that are met along the road. The legacy of the archaeological trip is not limited to the items and texts that were deciphered; rather, it becomes a tribute to the tenacity of human curiosity and the ongoing desire to comprehend our common history.

The mystery of the civilization that flourished in the Indus Valley is not only solved as the protagonist shares their discoveries with the rest of the globe; it also becomes a chapter in the greater narrative of the study of human history. The journey that the protagonist takes leaves a legacy that is not confined to academic journals; rather, it reverberates in the collective consciousness, serving as a source of inspiration for future generations of historians, archaeologists, and storytelling.

The archaeologist, who serves as our protagonist, emerges not only as a historian of the past but also as a storyteller, a seeker of truths, and a protector of cultural heritage. Their voyage into the enigma of the Indus Valley Civilization becomes a metaphor for the perennial human desire of understanding—an expedition that transcends the bounds of time and leaves an indelible mark on the tapestry of history. Following in the footsteps of the protagonist, we are also encouraged to participate in the journey, to peel back the layers of time, and to reveal the shadows that shroud the stories of those who came before us.

1.4 Uncover the initial clues pointing towards an untold story

Our narrative begins at the beginning of a captivating journey, which is initiated by the discovery of initial clues, which are cryptic fragments that point towards an untold story that is veiled in the shadows of history. This journey begins in the sun-soaked plains of the Indus Valley, where the whispers of an ancient civilization echo through the winds. Our protagonist is an ardent archaeologist who is set to solve the mystery that lies dormant beneath the layers of time. He is the driving force behind this archeological adventure.

The Mysterious Terrain:

The adventure starts against the backdrop of a mysterious terrain, which consists of expansive grasslands, riverbanks, and the silent ruins of a civilization that was once vibrant. An insatiable curiosity drives the protagonist to an archeological treasure trove, where the earth itself holds the forgotten history of an ancient people. The protagonist is lured to this treasure trove through an insatiable curiosity. The first hint can be found in the very earth that they are standing on, which is whispering secrets that have been dormant for millennia.

Not at all arbitrary is the selection of the location for the excavation. The findings are based on extensive research, satellite photography, and a profound comprehension of the intricacies that are associated with the geographical location. The protagonist, who is directed by a sense of intuition that has been honed by years of scholarly research, has the impression that this landscape is the path that leads to the discovery of a story that has been lost to the annals of time.

The Remnants of Silence:

As soon as the first spade makes contact with the surface of the earth, the relics of the past begin to become audible. The main character, who is surrounded by a group of devoted academics and archaeologists, takes in the sight of the worn bricks, pottery shards, and other remnants of an ancient world. The early clues are these mute witnesses to history, each of which carries the weight of a story that has not yet reached its conclusion.

As the archeological site is being meticulously documented, the process may now begin. Cataloging and analyzing each and every artifact, regardless of how seemingly trivial it may be, is done. The protagonist, armed with the tools of the trade, is aware that these shards contain the codes that would allow him to unlock the mysteries of a civilization that has been lost in the folds of time.

Artifacts as Symbols of Crypticism:

In the process of unearthing them, the protagonist discovers that the artifacts are not merely things but rather mysterious symbols that hint at a culture that is highly developed. Whether it be a little seal that is inscribed with complicated symbols, a piece of pottery that is covered with faded designs, or a statuette that is posed in a mysterious manner, each artifact contributes a new layer to the story that is being told. The early clues, the first whispers of a tongue that has been silent for a very long time, are contained in these lines.

The protagonist, who has been studying for a long time and has developed a keen eye, is able to discern patterns and symbols that go beyond the aesthetic significance. The existence of a motif that appears repeatedly, the meticulous arrangement of symbols on a seal, or the selection of materials that are used in the creation of an artifact are all examples of the early threads that are ready to be weaved into a tapestry awaiting completion.

The Mysterious Script:

The finding of a writing that was engraved onto seals, ceramics, and structures is a significant turning point in the story that is being told. As the protagonist comes face to face with a language that has not yet been deciphered, also known as a script, the mystery becomes even more complicated. This script is the key to revealing the mysteries of civilization. The challenge transforms into a journey to discover the undiscovered stories that are encoded inside the cryptic symbols, rather than merely an intellectual study.

Taking on the challenging endeavor of decipherment, the protagonist works together with linguists and other language specialists to accomplish this mission. With all of its loops and curves, the script presents itself as a puzzle that needs to be solved. The initial breakthroughs provide glimpses into the language landscape; nonetheless, the whole meaning of the script continues to be elusive, leaving the protagonist with the promise of a great epiphany.

The Marvels of Architecture and the Planning of Cities:

Beyond relics, the silent remnants include architectural marvels and urban planning of the ancient civilization. These are the things that have been left behind. A level of sophistication that challenges established beliefs is indicated by the arrangement of streets, the design of structures, and the presence of advanced drainage systems.

All of these elements lead to another level of sophistication. The first signs can be found not only in the majesty of the gigantic structures, but also in the precise organization of the urban landscape.

In the course of his exploration of the cityscape that emerges from beneath the layers of earth, the protagonist ponders the societal organization and governance mechanisms that made it possible for such urban design to occur. The clues are not limited to specific items; rather, they are woven into the very fabric of the city itself. They are the silent testament to a civilization that flourished in harmony with its surroundings.

Symbolic Art and Rituals: an Overview

As the protagonist dives deeper into the world of rituals and symbolic art, the mystery takes on a more profound quality. The rich tapestry of ideas and practices that may be seen in ceremonial items, religious statuettes, and depictions on ceramics is a fascinating discovery. The symbols that adorn these items become windows into the spiritual realm of the ancient civilization, leading towards stories of worship, rituals, and cultural expressions that have not been told before.

The protagonist, who has a deep respect for the holiness of these objects, makes an effort to comprehend the meaning that is contained inside them. Questions regarding the pantheon of deities, the significance of rituals, and the function of symbols in the process of establishing the cultural identity of the civilization are raised as a result of the earliest hints.

The Relationship Between Astronomical Alignments and Scientific Observation:

In the course of uncovering evidence of astronomical alignments and advanced mathematical comprehension, the protagonist discovers that the hidden story extends into the domain of scientific knowledge. The alignment of structures with astronomical phenomena, the precision with which time is measured, and the use of mathematical concepts in construction are all indications that the culture in question had a sophisticated awareness of the natural world.

The protagonist is prompted to reassess their preconceptions about the intellectual capacities of ancient peoples as a result of these revelations, which form the earliest clues. The story that has not yet been recounted takes into account not only the societal and cultural aspects, but also the scientific expertise that had a role in shaping the interaction that the civilization had with the universe.

Trade Routes and the Exchange of Cultural Ideas:

Evidence of trade routes and cultural interchange is brought to light, which causes the trip of the protagonist to stretch beyond the bounds of the dig site. The presence of items created from materials derived from other regions, seals portraying exotic creatures that are not local to the region, and the relics of a bustling market square are all indications of a society that is deeply connected with the wider world.

Reflections on the connectivity of ancient civilizations are sparked by the first indications of trade and cultural interchange. As the protagonist ponders the intercultural influences that played a role in the formation of the civilization, he or she begins to piece together a story of interaction that goes well beyond the territorial boundaries of the excavation site.

Identified Human Remains and the Dynamics of Society:

With the finding of human remains, the story that has not yet been told takes a dramatic and moving turn. A better understanding of the lives and dynamics of the ancient occupants can be gained through the examination of skeletal remains, burial patterns, and indications of societal hierarchies. While acknowledging the untold stories of individuals whose lives left permanent traces on the archaeological record, the protagonist attempts to come to terms with the humanity of the past.

The investigation of human remains turns out to be a gloomy but necessary component of the story. It is possible that the unwritten stories of individual lives, such as those of rulers, artisans, or ordinary residents, contribute to a more comprehensive knowledge of the fundamental social fabric of the civilization.

Changes in the Climate and Their Decline:

In the course of the protagonist's investigation of the trail of first clues, the story takes a turn toward the gloomy disclosure of climate change and the downfall of civilization. The evidence of environmental transformations, changes in river courses, and the impact of shifting climatic patterns become vital aspects of the story that have not yet been told.

The main character struggles with the knowledge that the decline of civilization was not entirely the consequence of internal issues but also a response to the obstacles provided by the natural environment. This is a realization that the protagonist struggles with. A civilization that is caught in the ebb and flow of environmental changes is now a part of the untold story, which contains both the resilience and fragility of the civilization.

In the process of unearthing first evidence, one does not follow a linear path but rather engages in a complex examination of the unseen tale of a society. In order to create a story that is timeless, every relic, script, architectural marvel, and scientific knowledge adds to the overall tale. In order to navigate the maze of history, the protagonist is led by an unrelenting desire for the past. As they peel back the layers of time, they uncover the shadows that cloak the forgotten stories of an ancient civilization.

The journey of the protagonist becomes a demonstration of the enduring human spirit of inquiry as the early clues come together to form a tapestry of revelations that are intertwined with one another. In the past, the untold story was left to the stillness of the past; but, because to the diligent work of the archaeologist, the story no longer remains silent. The excavation site, which was once a quiet witness to history, transforms into a stage where the hidden stories of an ancient civilization emerge from the shadows, allowing us to be witnesses to the echoes of the past.

Chapter 2

The Silent Ruins Speak

A deep discussion is taking place in the timeless embrace of the Indus Valley, where the sun sets long shadows across the quiet ruins of Mohenjo-Daro and Harappa. This conversation is a discourse between the past and the present, between the silent ruins and the hungry hearts of those who wish to comprehend. This tale digs into the core of this conversation, examining how the silent ruins communicate with one another. They resound with the sounds of an old symphony that beckons archaeologists, historians, and dreamers alike.

The Sounds of Bricks That Have Been Weathered:

There are worn bricks that spring from the ground like ancient sentinels at the center of the archaeological site. These bricks are bearing the weight of millennia. The silent remains, which were once filled with lively structures that contained the hopes and routines of a flourishing civilization, now stand as stoic witnesses to the passage of time. Every brick, every wall that has been precisely built out, contains within it the echoes of a time that has long since passed.

During the process of the archaeologist tracing the contours of these aged bricks, the tactile connection acts as a channel through which the silent ruins pass on their narrative. The flaws in the bricks tell stories about the artisans who fashioned them, the intricacies in construction hint at the architectural brilliance of the builders, and the sheer existence of these monuments becomes a testament to the fact that the civilization that once flourished here was able to persevere and survive.

The Fragmentation of Pottery into a Mosaic:

A mosaic of pottery shards is waiting to be discovered beneath the layers of earth; it is a tapestry that was woven by the hands of a people who have long since passed away. Now, the fragments, which were once a part of vessels that carried stories and nutrition, provide a look into the artistic expressions and daily lives of the ancient civilization. The silent ruins, through these shattered fragments, speak of culinary traditions, cultural aesthetics, and the underlying human drive to create.

The mosaic is pieced together by the archaeologist, who has a keen eye for detail and recognizes patterns, motifs, and the development of artistic forms.

Fragments of pottery become containers of memory, relaying the unwritten stories of communal meetings, trade transactions, and the cultural nuances encoded in the vessels that once graced the hands of the ancient inhabitants. These stories are lost to time.

The Script That Was Carved in Silence:

Discovered among the objects that have been uncovered is a script that has been engraved in silence and is currently waiting to be interpreted. The motionless ruins, which are studded with these mysterious symbols, become the canvas against which an ancient language is revealed. Archaeologists are drawn into the field of linguistic inquiry by the writing, which has been undeciphered for centuries. This mystery beckons them to investigate the script.

The protagonist, armed with various weapons of interpretation, dances with the screenplay in order to get the desired effect. Every single character, every single curve and line, reverberates with the ability to reveal the stories that are concealed behind the silent ruins. A connection is created between the contemporary investigator and the ancient voices that once communicated through these symbols through the use of the script, which is a type of written communication that has been frozen in time.

The Reverberations of Urban Planning:

The still ruins are not only strewn remnants; rather, they are organized symphonies of urban planning. A civilization that understood the choreography of city life would have streets that were planned out in careful grids, drainage systems that were created with foresight, and structures that rose from the soil in multiple stories. All of these elements echo the harmonic order of a civilization. The layout of the city, which was previously bustling with activity, now echoes the footsteps of its former inhabitants, but the city itself is now quiet.

As the archaeologist makes their way through these planned streets, the silent ruins reveal not just the physical architecture but also the socio political and economic factors that were responsible for shaping the urban landscape. In addition, the planned design of public areas hints at a collective spirit that reverberated through the streets of antiquity. The absence of evident hierarchical structures raises issues about the egalitarian nature of the society, and other questions are raised regarding the nature of the civilization.

The resonance of artistic expression:

Sculptures, figures, and carvings that were previously used to decorate the cityscape are brought to light amidst the silent ruins. These are the relics of artistic expression to be found. These artifacts, which have been preserved from the beginning of time, provide insight into the aesthetic tastes, religious beliefs, and socioeconomic values of the ancient society.

By virtue of the creative vestiges that they contain, the silent ruins have been transformed into galleries that exhibit the inventiveness and spirituality of a people who have been lost to history.

By being sensitive to the subtleties of artistic expression, the archaeologist is able to analyze the meaning contained within each sculpture, contemplate the stance of figurines, and think about the rituals or narratives that these figurines might represent. The silent ruins, by virtue of the creative relics that they contain, transcend the material and invite the investigator to see the echoes of the inner world of an ancient culture.

The Spiritual Reverberations of Artifacts Used in Rituals:

Artifacts that speak not just of daily life but also of the spiritual realm can be found within the ruins that are silent. These artifacts are a complex dance of ritual artifacts, symbolism, and ceremonial locations. The silent echoes of religious rites, which were previously heard resonating through the temples and sanctuaries, now find resonance in the artifacts that have been left behind. In the ancient society, these items, whether they be religious statuettes or ritualistic seals, become conduits to the spiritual qualities of the civilization.

During the process of the archaeologist uncovering these ritual items, a spiritual conversation takes place. Through the use of these artifacts, the quiet ruins tell stories about worship, ceremonies, and the close relationship that exists between the earthly and the holy. The investigator transforms into a seeker of spiritual truths when they are in the company of these artifacts. They begin to piece together the unwritten stories of a civilization's search for transcendence.

The harmony of scientific understanding:

proof of mathematical prowess, astronomical alignments, and a profound interaction with the natural world can be found beneath the silent ruins. These signs of scientific understanding also include proof of astronomical alignments. Artifacts, structures, and meticulous measurements that were left behind are the silent echoes of scientific investigation that continue to reverberate through the world. Through its eerie remains, the old civilization becomes a living testimony to the harmonious relationship that exists between the human mind and the natural world.

Through the process of deciphering these scientific harmonies, the archaeologist is able to reveal the previously unknown stories of a people who navigated the cosmos with precision and considered the secrets of the universe. The silent ruins, with their astronomical alignments and mathematical complexity, serve as a bridge between the intellectual pursuits of the past and the inquisitive spirit of the present.

A Crossroads for the Exchange of Businesses and Cultures:

There is evidence of trade routes and cultural interchange in the quiet ruins, which lends credence to the idea that there was a civilization that existed at the intersection of the ancient world. The cosmopolitan nature of the ancient people is revealed by the artifacts, materials imported from faraway locations, and portrayals of strange motifs that are found in all of these items. Stories of economic life and cultural diversity are told through the quiet ruins, which consist of the relics of marketplaces and trading hubs.

The silent ruins become gates to untold stories of merchants, travelers, and the bustling exchanges that once energized the streets as the archaeologist finds these traces of cross-cultural contacts. These traces are being discovered during the course of the excavation. The investigator transforms into a witness to the echoes of a civilization that is engaged in a dance of cultural reciprocity while at the same time being surrounded by artifacts that have a distant origin.

The Buried Lives of People and the Narratives of Society:

Not only do the quiet ruins contain artifacts and architecture, but they also contain the stories of lives lived, loves lost, and societal narratives that were inscribed into the very fabric of the ancient civilization. Human bones, burial traditions, and evidence of societal hierarchy provide a moving peek into the daily struggles and victories of a people whose stories have been muted by the passage of time on account of the passage of time.

Through the process of unearthing these buried lives, the archaeologist becomes a guardian of the untold stories of persons who once strolled the streets of the ancient city as they were being discovered. Through the poignant vestiges of human existence, the quiet ruins speak of the resiliency, aspirations, and intricacies of a society that has been sewn into the fabric of its own history.

The Environmental Whispers and the Unspoken Decline of the Environment:

As the story progresses, the silent ruins tell the unspoken story of decline. This is a story that is connected with the whispers of environmental shifts and the obstacles that the ancient civilization had to overcome. There is evidence of a society that is caught in the ebb and flow of nature's forces, as evidenced by the changing river courses, environmental degradation, and the impact of climatic oscillations.

The archaeologist, who is sensitive to the environmental mutterings that are whispered amid the silent ruins, ponders the lessons that are timeless.

Not only does the demise of civilization become a historical event, but it also becomes a cautionary tale, advising the current generation to pay attention to the echoes of environmental changes and the impact that human actions have on the longevity of civilizations.

During the dance that takes place between the investigator and the silent ruins, an ancient symphony is being performed. This symphony is a complex composition of daily life, cultural expressions, spiritual pursuits, and scientific investigations. The silent ruins, despite the fact that they do not contain any spoken words, transform into eloquent storytellers, crafting a narrative that goes beyond the confines of time. When the artifacts are unearthed and the symbols are deciphered by the archaeologist, they transform into conduits that allow the quiet ruins to communicate in a language that is beyond the centuries.

We are beckoned to listen and learn by the sounds of an ancient symphony that are emanating from the ruins that cannot be heard. In doing so, they encourage us to reflect on the human experience throughout time and space, to acknowledge the connectivity of civilizations, and to be witnesses to the resilience and fragility that are sewn into the fabric of history. When we are in the midst of the quiet ruins, we, too, become participants in this eternal conversation. We embrace the echoes of an ancient symphony that reverberates down the halls of the past.

2.1 Explore the ancient ruins of Mohenjo-Daro and Harappa

In the endless and sun-drenched plains of the Indian subcontinent, where the river once flowed with life and the remnants of an old civilization remain, the quiet cities of Mohenjo-Daro and Harappa stand as mysterious testaments to a bygone period. Both of these towns are located in the region of the Indian subcontinent. When one sets out on a journey to investigate these ancient ruins, it seems as if one is traveling through the passageways of time and following in the footsteps of a people who once flourished along the banks of the powerful Indus River. As we travel further into the heart of the Indus Valley Civilization, this story will reveal the intricate web of history, culture, and mystery that has been woven over its whole.

The mysterious beginnings of the story:

The journey starts at the point where the ancient ruins of Mohenjo-Daro and Harappa are just beginning to emerge from the dust that has accumulated over the course of centuries. Archaeologists, historians, and interested travelers are invited to explore these preserved cities, which date back to the third millennium before the common era (BCE), in order to uncover the mysteries that are concealed within their aged walls. The mysterious beginnings of these communities laid the groundwork for a voyage that took place over the course of millennia.

Both Mohenjo-Daro, which literally means "Mound of the Dead," and Harappa, which is named after the current town that is located nearby, were once prosperous urban sites of the Indus Valley Civilization but have since been abandoned. Contemporary with ancient Mesopotamia and Egypt, the civilization itself featured extensive urban planning, sophisticated architecture, and a level of technological skill that contradicted common ideas of ancient societies. It was also contemporary with ancient Egypt.

The urban marvels of Mohenjo-Daro:

As soon as we enter the tranquil city of Mohenjo-Daro, the urban marvels begin to reveal themselves. The layout of the city, which includes well-planned streets, advanced drainage systems, and multistory buildings, demonstrates a degree of urban sophistication that is comparable to, and in some respects surpasses, that of many current civilizations. It is a testament to the excellent engineering skills of those who constructed the Great Bath, which is a massive reservoir that stands as an architectural marvel because of its size.

As one makes their way through the meticulously laid out streets of Mohenjo-Daro, one can hear the reverberations of an ancient communal way of life. It is clear from the living quarters, granaries, and public places that the society in question placed a high emphasis on order, cleanliness, and the general well-being of the community. Explorers are now being invited to decode the histories that have been inscribed into the foundations of the city by the quiet stones, which were previously witnesses to the hum of daily life.

The mysteries surrounding Harappa:

When it comes to the splendor of the Indus Valley Civilization, Harappa, which is located in the Punjab region of Pakistan at the present time, is on par with Mohenjo-Daro. When explorers step foot on the ancient land of Harappa, the mysteries of the city, along with those of its sister city, begin to reveal themselves. The meticulously organized grid of streets, the intricate architecture, and the remnants of a busy marketplace all point to a city that flourished as a result of its commercial activity, cultural activities, and innovative ideas.

The archaeological ruins of Harappa reveal layers upon layers of history, with each strata preserving bits of pottery, tools, and artifacts that weave a tapestry of ancient life. Harappa is located in the northwestern region of India. Even though it is silent, the city tells stories of trading, craftsmanship, and a society that interacted with the rest of the globe through complex trade networks.

The Unspoken Conversations That Make Up Everyday Life:

As our exploration of the silent ruins of Mohenjo-Daro and Harappa continues, remains of daily life begin to emerge from the dust that has accumulated over the course of many years.

The shards of pottery, delicately crafted utensils, and tools that are dispersed around the sites become the silent murmurs of activities that once filled the streets and homes of these ancient towns once upon a time.

The discovery of a granary in Mohenjo-Daro is indicative of careful urban design and an awareness of the importance of agricultural sustainability. The uniform bricks, each of which bears the signature of a sophisticated construction technique, are indicative of a culture that placed a high emphasis on precision and longevity. The relics provide a look into the routines, crafts, and familial bonds that characterized the ancient Indus Valley Civilization. These artifacts resonate with the faint whispers of daily life that occur in these cities.

The Mysterious Script:

The existence of a script, which is a written language that, despite decades of scientific labor, has not been deciphered, is one of the lingering mysteries that continue to interest explorers of Mohenjo-Daro and Harappa. The mysterious script is found on seals, ceramics, and structures, and it has left archaeologists and linguists with a tantalizing problem that has not yet been completely solved.

Through the inscriptions that have been etched into the stones of the silent ruins, explorers are being beckoned to uncover the mysteries of the ancient script. There is a possibility that the intellectual, spiritual, and societal aspects of the civilization could be revealed through the symbols, geometric patterns, and characters that become gateways to a language. In the same way that a silent sentinel watches over the untold stories of Mohenjo-Daro and Harappa, the mysterious script does the same.

The Relationship Between Religious Activities and Creative Expressions:

There is evidence of artistic expressions and religious rituals that can be found among the silent ruins. These traces provide views into the spiritual dimensions of the Indus Valley Civilization. Figurines that show deities or legendary beings, exquisite carvings on seals, and artifacts used in ceremonies are all indications of a people that participated in elaborate rituals and decorated their surroundings with symbolic art.

There is a sense of the hallowed that is evoked by the hushed murmurs of religious practices that are carried out in Mohenjo-Daro and Harappa. When it comes to understanding the spiritual worldview of the ancient people, the images of animals, the seated figures in meditation poses, and the precise arrangement of symbols on seals all become conduits for this understanding. The silent ruins, by virtue of the creative relics that they contain, transcend the material and urge explorers to consider the intangible parts of the belief system that was prevalent in an ancient society.

Commercial and Cultural Interactions:

Once explorers make their way through the ancient alleyways of Mohenjo-Daro and Harappa, they discover evidence of trade and cultural interaction that have been left behind. The artifacts, which include seals depicting animals that are not endemic to the area, provide evidence of a civilization that was involved in extensive trading networks. Through these relics, the silent ruins become gates to stories that have not been told before about the economic life, cross-cultural contacts, and cosmopolitan nature of the ancient cities.

The marketplace, with its evidence of weights and measures, becomes a testimonial to the economic acumen of the civilization that is being discussed. There is a cultural wealth that transcends geographical limits, as seen by the objects that were crafted from materials that were gathered from other islands. The hushed remains, which were once bustling centers of commerce and cultural exchange, invite travelers to imagine the dynamic exchanges that once characterized the old streets.

Human Remains and Lives That Have Been Buried:

Untold tales of lives lived, loves lost, and societal narratives engraved into the very fabric of the ancient society are hidden beneath the layers of earth that cover the silent remains. These stories are buried beneath the layers of soil. There are heartbreaking glimpses into the daily hardships and accomplishments of a people whose stories have been muted by time that can be found in human bones, burial traditions, and traces of society hierarchies.

When burial sites are excavated, it becomes an opportunity to conduct an in-depth investigation into the people who once strolled the streets of Mohenjo-Daro and Harappa. Through the poignant vestiges of human existence, the quiet ruins speak of the resiliency, aspirations, and intricacies of a society that has been sewn into the fabric of its own history. The stories of people whose lives left permanent impressions on the archaeological record are revealed when archaeologists carefully dig these buried lives. The towns that have been silent for centuries are the source of these stories.

The Fall and Its Repercussions upon the Environment:

A storyline that is intertwined with the whispers of environmental shifts and obstacles faced by the ancient society is revealed as the narrative progresses, and the quiet ruins are a witness to the unsaid story of decline. There is evidence of a society that is caught in the ebb and flow of nature's forces, as evidenced by the changing river courses, environmental degradation, and the impact of climatic oscillations.

A era of transition and decline is hinted at by the silent ruins, which are composed of the relics of abandoned constructions and altered city layouts.

The once-thriving cities, which are now quiet witnesses to the passage of time, provoke reflective thought about the susceptibilities of civilizations in the face of changes in the environment. The echoes of an environmental narrative that can be found inside Mohenjo-Daro and Harappa become a profound reflection on the fragile balance that exists between human cultures and the natural world.

The Importance of Preserving it and Its Contemporary Significance:

As we come to the end of our investigation of the ancient ruins of Mohenjo-Daro and Harappa, the subject of preservation and the importance of these historical sites in the modern day arises. In spite of the fact that time has ravaged them, the silent cities continue to be significant cultural heritage sites that provide glimpses into the distant past. Archaeologists, conservationists, and members of the local community all make significant contributions to the ongoing preservation of these enigmatic ruins through their careful efforts.

Mohenjo-Daro and Harappa are ancient civilizations that have a modern significance that goes beyond the domain of academia. These locations, which have been declared as UNESCO World Heritage Sites, are regularly visited by people from all over the world. Reflections on the shared human legacy, the intricacies of urban life, and the lessons that history gives to both the current generation and the generations to come are prompted by the silent ruins, which have an enchantment that has stood strong for centuries.

The examination of the ancient remains of Mohenjo-Daro and Harappa is like going on a voyage through time; it is an expedition that reveals the hushed utterances of a remarkable civilization. Contemporary explorers are invited to become guardians of a common human legacy by virtue of the streets, structures, artifacts, and untold stories that are concealed within these quiet cities. These cities transcend the limits of the past.

As we walk on the old ground, we are able to hear the echoes of daily life, the mysteries of a script that has not been decoded, the abundance of artistic expressions, and the intricacies of the dynamics of society. In their stoic presence, the silent ruins offer conduits for understanding the spiritual, economic, and cultural components of the civilization that flourished in the Indus Valley.

Mohenjo-Daro and Harappa are not simply a journey into antiquity; rather, it is an endeavor to bridge the temporal gap, to listen to the whispers of the past, and to weave the threads of old narratives into the fabric of our collective human story.

This is what the exploration of these two ancient sites is all about. It is possible that the stones in the towns of Mohenjo-Daro and Harappa do not communicate in words; yet, they do echo with a language that is not bound by time; a language that invites us to investigate, reflect, and appreciate the eternal heritage of the Indus Valley Civilization.

2.2 Descriptions of the advanced urban planning, drainage systems, and artifacts

The relics of advanced urban design, inventive drainage systems, and mysterious artifacts whisper tales of an ancient marvel known as the Indus Valley society. These remnants may be found in the sun-soaked plains of the Indian subcontinent, namely in the region where the Indus River once nurtured a sophisticated society. During the time period of around 3300 BCE to 1300 BCE, this flourishing civilization was on par with its contemporaries in Mesopotamia and Egypt. It left behind silent testimony to its inventiveness and the cultural wealth it possessed. We are about to start on a voyage through the corridors of time as we unravel the complexities of urban design, the brilliance of drainage systems, and the mysteries that are embedded in artifacts.

Mohenjo-Daro and Harappa: A Symphony of Order in Advanced Urban Planning: What We Can Learn from These Cities

Mohenjo-Daro and Harappa, both of which have been left in ruins, are witnesses to an urban planning achievement that is without precedent. A level of order and organization that defies conventional conceptions of early urban settlements is reflected in the layouts of these ancient cities, which were meticulously built with a grid-like network of streets.

Places of Architecture and Streets:

In instance, the streets of Mohenjo-Daro were organized in a grid that was extremely exact, demonstrating a sophisticated awareness of the cardinal directions.

A well-organized urban fabric was created by the intersection of wide avenues at right angles. The buildings, which were built using bricks that were standardized, displayed a pattern of uniformity that suggested that careful planning and construction processes were utilized.

The residential sections, which were made up of structures with multiple stories, gave the impression that the society had a strong knowledge of the importance of space efficiency. It was possible to infer that these buildings, some of which featured private baths, exhibited a level of living that was advanced for the time period. There are stories to be told about a society that flourished in tune with its surroundings, and the silent ruins, with their well-organized streets and architectural marvels, tell those stories.

Areas Open to the Public and Amenities:

It is a monument to the civilization's expertise of urban planning that the Great Bath of Mohenjo-Daro stands as a significant landmark. Not only did this enormous reservoir function as a communal bathing area, but it also served as a symbol of social togetherness and shared rituals within the community. Its intricate engineering for water supply and drainage was a testament to its significance. The existence of public places that have been properly planned demonstrates an awareness of the significance of communal life and the facilities that are provided by the government.

The Zoning of Commercial and Residential Areas:

The zoning of Mohenjo-Daro and Harappa indicated a level of urban sophistication that distinguished between residential and commercial zones. This was done in order to attract tourists. The existence of granaries was indicative of a sophisticated approach to the management of resources and information storage. Through their meticulously zoned layout, the silent ruins speak of a culture that valued not only the functional aspects of urban living but also the aesthetic and communal features of urban living.

A technological marvel from antiquity, the ingenious drainage systems consist of:

A number of the civilizations that existed during the same time period as the Indus Valley Civilization are not as technologically advanced as the drainage systems that they developed. A complex network of drains and sewage systems was developed by the ancient engineers of Mohenjo-Daro and Harappa. This network demonstrated an understanding of hydraulics and urban sanitation that was unmatched during their time period when it was constructed.

Intelligent Wastewater Treatment Systems:

The dwellings in Mohenjo-Daro were equipped with individual restrooms and toilets that were linked to a complex system of underground drains. The construction of these drains was meticulously done with bricks that interlocked with one another, and also contained manholes allowing access to maintenance. The sophisticated sewage systems, which were constructed with a gradual slope for the purpose of efficient waste disposal, were a monument to the advanced engineering knowledge that the residents possessed.

Sanitation in Urban Areas and Public Health:

The existence of drainage systems that were thoughtfully built was evidence of a dedication to maintaining urban cleanliness and public health. In Mohenjo-Daro and Harappa, the advanced sanitation methods contributed to a healthier living environment, lowering the danger of waterborne diseases and enhancing the overall well-being of the community. This was accomplished by reducing the frequency of waterborne infections. The silent remains, with their concealed conduits, tell the narrative of a society that placed a high priority on the hygiene and health of its metropolitan areas.

Measures to Manage Stormwater:

The drainage systems were not only concerned with the disposal of sewage; in addition to that, they included provisions for the management of stormwater. Throughout the streets of Mohenjo-Daro, there were drains that were created in such a way that they effectively diverted rainwater away from the central business district. This dual-functionality demonstrated a degree of urban design that took into consideration the various issues that are provided by both garbage from the home and elements from the natural environment.

Mysterious Artifacts: Symbols of Mysterious Meanings and Questions That Remain Unanswered:

The archaeological excavations that were conducted at Mohenjo-Daro and Harappa resulted in the discovery of a treasure trove of artifacts. Each of these objects was a testament to the cultural and intellectual wealth of the civilization that was being studied. Nevertheless, among these relics, there was one enigma that remained unsolved: the script that was adorning seals, ceramics, and structures that had not been determined.

This is the Mysterious Writer:

Even though the script of the Indus Valley Civilization has been the subject of scholarly interest for decades, it continues to be a mystery that needs to be solved. The writing, which is etched onto seals and artifacts, is made up of a collection of symbols and characters that have not been able to be deciphered. In spite of the fact that they have a large number of objects that feature this writing, linguists and archaeologists have not yet been able to decipher its linguistic code.

In the form of these mysterious inscriptions, the silent ruins invite scholars to decipher the messages that were once an essential component of the intellectual history of the civilization. Because of the geometric perfection of the symbols, it is possible that they were used in a form of written communication that had administrative, religious, or cultural importance.

Art that is Symbolic:

In addition to the written language, the items that were discovered at Mohenjo-Daro and Harappa contained a wonderful variety of symbolic artwork. Animals, figures from mythology, and elaborate patterns were carved into seals, and these carvings provided a glimpse into the creative and spiritual leanings of the society. Through the use of these symbolic items, the silent ruins provide an opportunity for reflection on the cultural symbols and rituals that formerly characterized the daily life of the ancient people.

Employing Craftsmanship and Utility:

Symbolic or sacred things were not the only types of artifacts that were produced by the Indus Valley Civilization. These artifacts also included utilitarian pieces that displayed a high level of craftsmanship. An example of this would be pottery, which contained elaborate designs and a manufacturing method that was uniform. Objects such as tools, implements, and ornaments were indicative of a civilization that placed equal importance on aesthetics and functionality.

Artifacts as Testimonies to Trade: Crossroads of Cultural Exchange

The items that were found in Mohenjo-Daro and Harappa offer insights into the massive trade networks that connected the civilization with territories that were located in the far reaches of the world. The cosmopolitan aspect of the Indus Valley Civilization is demonstrated by the presence of seals that portray animals that were not indigenous to the nearby environment, exotic materials that were procured from a great distance, and depictions of cultural motifs that originated from diverse places.

Trade Routes and Materials of Uncommon Origin:

The existence of objects that were crafted from materials such as lapis lazuli and carnelian, which were not readily available in the area, provided evidence of a flourishing trading network that extended to countries such as Mesopotamia and Central Asia. These exotic materials, which were painstakingly sculpted into objects, were a testament to the economic vigor and cross-cultural interactions that were characteristic of the ancient cities.

Some Indicators of the Diversity of Cultures:

Mohenjo-Daro and Harappa artifacts, with their many influences and styles, provided evidence of a culture that valued and celebrated the existence of a vast range of cultural traditions. A mixing of creative traditions was suggested by the depictions on seals and pottery, which had an effect on the aesthetics and symbols that were utilized in the artifacts. With the help of these artifacts, the quiet ruins tell the narrative of a civilization that existed at a crossroads of cultural exchange, where ideas, materials, and influences freely flowed.

Artifacts of Ritual Value: An Investigation into the Spiritual Dimension:

Artifacts that offer insights into the spiritual qualities of the civilization can be found lying dormant within the ruins of Mohenjo-Daro and Harappa. Artifacts such as ritualistic seals, figurines, and ceremonial objects provide insight into the spiritual worldview of the ancient occupants. These artifacts speak of a people who engaged in intricate religious rites.

Sealings used in rituals:

The complex carvings of animals, anthropomorphic figures, and symbols that were found on the seals that were uncovered in the archaeological sites show that there is a relationship to religious or ritualistic activity. The presence of these seals, which are frequently discovered in conjunction with funerals, provides evidence of a religious system that put significance on the afterlife or spiritual realms. With the help of these seals, the silent ruins create an atmosphere that is conducive to supposition regarding the ceremonies and rituals that were formerly performed within the ancient towns.

As well as Figurines and Sculptures:

Examples of the artifacts include sculptures and figurines that depict anthropomorphic representations of deities, legendary entities, and other supernatural beings. An artistic sense that tries to capture the spiritual essence of the subjects is shown in the painstaking craftsmanship of these artifacts, which expresses a reverence for the divine. After being adorned with these religious relics, the ruins that were before silent have become sacred spaces that once reverberated with the echoes of old activities.

The expression of artistic creativity through ceramics, figurines, and aesthetic nuances:

Evidence of a sophisticated level of artistic expression may be seen in the pottery and figurines that were found in Mohenjo-Daro and Harappa. The objects, with their detailed designs, themes, and craftsmanship, give a vivid picture of a culture that valued not only the practical aspects of everyday life but also the aesthetic nuances that were present in those aspects.

The Art of Pottery as a Concept:

Evidence of the artistic sensibility of the people who lived in the Indus Valley Civilization can be found in the pottery that they produced. Various objects, including bowls, jars, and vessels, were embellished with elaborate designs, geometric patterns, and animal decorations. It was suggested that the production of pottery had reached a degree of artistry and industrial organization, both of which contributed to the cultural identity of the civilization.

Artworks of Sculpture and Figurines:

The archeological sites yielded a wide variety of figurines, ranging from miniature statuettes of humans to portrayals of animals. In addition to demonstrating a mastery of sculptural skills, these objects demonstrated a thorough awareness of form. With their intricate facial characteristics and poses, the humanoid sculptures gave the impression that they were artistic depictions of people or gods. Through the use of these figurines, the silent ruins are transformed into galleries that preserve the aesthetic preferences and creative expressions of a civilization that has been lost to the passage of time.

Scientific Investigations and the Alignments of Astronomical Objects:

Evidence of scientific investigation and astronomical alignments can be found beneath the silent remains of Mohenjo-Daro and Harappa, which sheds information on the intellectual activities of the civilization. A society that has a great awareness of the natural world is demonstrated by the objects and structures on display, which are characterized by their mathematical precision and alignment with the celestial bodies.

Absolute Accuracy in Mathematics:

Bricks that were standardized and utilized in the construction of Mohenjo-Daro and Harappa provided evidence of a sophisticated understanding of geometry and measurement. These bricks have regular ratios and measurements, which suggests that they are part of a standardized system of measurement. This reveals an advanced degree of mathematical knowledge, which contributed to the precision in urban planning and building.

Aspects of Astronomical Alignment:

There is a strong indication that people are aware of astronomical occurrences since certain structures are oriented in such a way that they align with celestial events like solstices. An example of this would be the Great Bath of Mohenjo-Daro, which displays alignments with key solar events. These deliberate alignments are indicative of a society that not only studied the cosmos but also included celestial factors into the design of its buildings. With their astronomical echoes, the silent ruins transform into observatories that once united the people who lived there with the rhythmic dance of the celestial bodies.

Through the investigation of the sophisticated urban planning, creative drainage systems, and mysterious artifacts of the Indus Valley Civilization, we are able to unravel a tapestry that is woven with threads of ingenuity, mystery, and cultural wealth. In the silent ruins of Mohenjo-Daro and Harappa, with their perfectly organized cities, intricate drainage networks, and various artifacts, we are given the opportunity to gain a glimpse into the complexity of an ancient society that flourished along the banks of the Indus River.

The advanced urban design of Mohenjo-Daro and Harappa, which is marked by organized streets, zoned structures, and communal amenities, speaks of a society that prioritized not only the utilitarian aspects of its inhabitants' lives but also the aesthetics and well-being of those who lived there. These inventive drainage systems, which feature advanced sewage disposal and stormwater management, are evidence of a technological prowess that has helped to the creation of a healthy urban environment.

The mysterious items, which are embellished with a writing that cannot be understood, symbolic art, and representations of spiritual beliefs, continue to generate a sense of mystery that will continue to exist till the current day. The artifacts provide evidence of a civilization that located itself at a crossroads of cultural exchange and was involved in trading networks that extended to far-flung locations. The artistic expressions, whether they are in the form of figurines, ceramics, or religious artifacts, provide glimpses into the creative and spiritual aspects of everyday life.

The scientific investigation that is entrenched in mathematical accuracy and astronomical alignments adds another element to the narrative that is being told about the ruins of Mohenjo-Daro and Harappa, which are currently remaining mute. It gives the impression of a civilization that endeavored to comprehend the natural world by setting its constructions in harmony with the occurrences of the heavens and utilizing mathematical concepts in the process of urban design.

There is a universe where the echoes of ingenuity and cultural richness bounce across the millennia, and as we ponder these silent ruins, we are lured into that world. Artifacts, roadways, and drainage systems become pieces of a civilization that once flourished in the embrace of the Indus River. This civilization thrived in the region of South Asia. Exploration of these wonders transcends the borders of time, inviting us to marvel at the inventiveness of our ancient ancestors and to consider the mysteries that still remain within the silent corridors of Mohenjo-Daro and Harappa. These marvels have been discovered by humans.

2.3 Unearth the first fragments of a forgotten language

An expedition to excavate the first shards of a language that has been forgotten exists within the world of archeology, where the dust of eons rests upon silent ruins. This is a profound search. The narrative progresses as explorers, armed with trowels and brushes, dive into the ancient soil in search of remains of a linguistic legacy that has been hidden by the passage of time. It is a voyage that transcends the borders of history and linguistics, weaving together strands of mystery, perseverance, and the insatiable human need for information. The journey to rediscover a language that has been forgotten.

The Mystery of the Ruins Under the Silence:

The silent ruins, which are dispersed across the archeological landscape, hold within their weathered stones the echoes of a language that has been lost and forgotten since ancient times. Archaeologists, linguists, and language enthusiasts are compelled to embark on a trip that aims to unlock the doors to a linguistic realm that has been vanished in the past because of the mystery surrounding these silent vestiges.

In the sacred halls of Mohenjo-Daro, Harappa, and other ancient sites, the stones themselves transform into tablets, waiting in silence to reveal the secrets of a language that once reverberated through the bustling streets and public spaces of the old world. Exploration begins when explorers look at the inscriptions, symbols, and characters that are etched into the very fabric of the quiet ruins. This is the beginning of the journey to unearth the first remnants of this vanished language.

Silent Witnesses to the Past:

The script, which is a collection of symbols and characters that have been painstakingly etched into seals, pottery, and other structures, acts as a silent witness to a decipherable language code that is currently waiting to be discovered. A complex method of written communication that once flourished in the ancient civilization is suggested by the fact that the first pieces of the language that has been forgotten have been discovered in the mysterious script.

Archaeologists are uncovering these inscriptions with great care, and the atmosphere is filled with awe and suspense during this process. Each symbol that is etched into the stones becomes a time capsule, holding the thoughts, tales, and expressions of a people who lived thousands of years ago. In spite of the fact that it is silent, the script functions as a connection between the contemporary investigator and the language tapestry of generations gone by.

The Linguistic Puzzle: Deciphering the Narratives That Have Not Been Written Down:

The linguistic conundrum that is presented by the language that has been lost evokes a chorus of queries that seem to resound across the halls of academic institutions. How do these symbols represent the phonetic values of the language? What are the grammatical structures that are involved in the language? Is it a linguistic system that exists in isolation or is it affiliated with a larger language family? The desire to decipher the unwritten narratives that are embedded in the script is propelled by these questions, which are reverberating through the cognitive processes of linguists.

Linguistic detectives, equipped with comparative analysis, contextual clues, and a comprehensive understanding of the evolution of language, initially begin to piece together the pieces of the language that has been forgotten. The script, which was long considered an indecipherable code, transforms into a mosaic that is waiting to be recreated. It is a linguistic Rosetta Stone that holds the promise of unlocking the stories, poems, and records of an ancient society.

A Comparative Linguistics Approach to the Investigation of Ancestral Roots:

Comparative linguistics is a strategy that makes links between the language that has been forgotten and other linguistic systems that are already known.

Linguists use comparative linguistics tools in order to decipher the language. When compared to languages that have a similar historical background or are located in close proximity to one another geographically, the initial fragments provide indications about the likely linguistic family to which the language that has been forgotten belongs.

Beginning to take shape is the delicate dance of phonetic similarities, grammatical structures, and lexical cognates involved in the process. While the linguistic trail is not particularly strong, it does create tentative linkages to languages spoken in nearby regions and traces the roots of ancestor languages. For the purpose of reviving the language that has been forgotten, the procedure transforms into a linguistic voyage that spans both time and distance, as linguists negotiate the complex maze of linguistic evolution.

The Cultural Tapestry: Unraveling the Contextual Insights of the Situation

Archaeologists are providing contextual insights taken from the cultural tapestry of the old society, which is allowing the first shards of the language that has been forgotten to obtain depth and meaning. Not only do the inscriptions offer linguistic expressions, but they also show cultural nuances, religious beliefs, and society practices when they are evaluated in conjunction with archeological findings.

An increasingly detailed story is being revealed when explorers find objects that are embellished with the lettering. When it comes to deciphering the mysteries of language, the context in which the phrase was used, whether it be in administrative documents, religious ceremonies, or everyday communications, becomes an essential key. The language that has been forgotten, which was once a mysterious conundrum, now gives life to the ruins that have been rendered silent, making it possible for the stories of the past to be told once more.

The Rosetta Stone: A Key to the Language That Has Been Forgotten

A tangible artifact that has inscriptions in several languages, a linguistic Rosetta Stone becomes a beacon of hope in the search to interpret the forgotten language. It serves as a bridge between the known and the unknown, creating a connection between the two. The Rosetta Stone, whether it is a real item or a metaphorical construction, becomes a key to open the linguistic door that separates modern researchers from the old script. This door provides access to the ancient script.

With the Rosetta Stone in their possession, linguists are able to compare the inscriptions in the language that has been forgotten with those in a language that is already known. The shared portions, which act as anchor points, make the process of deciphering easier to accomplish.

After being cloaked in mystery for a long time, the first bits of the forgotten language are now finding resonance in the parts that have been translated, which brings the linguistic riddle closer to being finished.

The Resurrected Language: A Symphony of Voices from the Past:

There is a sense of accomplishment and revelation that permeates the academic landscape as the linguistic journey continues to develop and the first bits of the language that has been forgotten are stitched together. It is a symphony of voices from the past that are reverberating through the halls of time, and the language, which was once banished to the silent ruins, has been once again brought back to life.

By deciphering the language that had been forgotten, the grammar, syntax, and vocabulary of the language are revealed. A strong sense of success is experienced by linguists as they describe the language norms that regulated ancient writing. Despite the fact that it has been silent for millennia, the resurrected language becomes a living witness to the tenacity of linguistic research and the unquenchable desire of humans to comprehend the past.

Obstacles and Debates: Finding Your Way Through the Linguistic Labyrinth:

The journey to recover the initial bits of a language that has been forgotten is not without its difficulties and there are debates involved. Many times, scholarly arguments are held over linguistic reconstructions, and these debates frequently involve contrasting interpretations and conflicting theories. Additional challenges are presented by the fact that there is no live group that speaks the language, which means that the nuances of pronunciation and usage are still speculated upon.

Methods of decipherment, historical linguistics, and the veracity of postulated linguistic linkages are all contentious topics that could potentially create disagreements. A thorough scholarship, collaboration across disciplines, and a readiness to reevaluate hypotheses in light of new evidence are all necessary components of the process of resurrecting a language that has been forgotten.

The Importance of the Present: Going Beyond the Boundaries of Academics to Cultural Heritage:

The rediscovery of a language that had been forgotten exceeds the bounds of academic study; it carries present importance that extends to encompass cultural legacy and communal identity. The resurrected language functions as a cultural bridge, bridging the gap between contemporary societies and their historical precedents. The ability of speakers of today to interact with the linguistic legacy left by their ancestors is one of the ways in which it helps to cultivate a sense of continuity and belonging.

Outside of the realm of linguistic circles, the modern significance of a revived language is reflected in the efforts that are being made to revitalize cultural traditions. When it comes to maintaining and commemorating the linguistic heritage that was uncovered from the quiet ruins, language revival projects, educational activities, and community engagement become essential components.

The journey to excavate the earliest fragments of a language that has been forgotten unfolds as a linguistic odyssey across time as it takes place in the shadows of the quiet ruins. The script, which was originally thought to be incomprehensible, has now transformed into a story that is eager to be read. The linguistic jigsaw, which is stitched together through comparative research and contextual insights, shows the intricate tapestry of the language used by an ancient society.

The story of human curiosity and resiliency is woven together by the victories and obstacles, controversies and revelations that occur throughout the narrative. The long-lost language, which had been relegated to the forgotten halls of history, has been brought back to life, resulting in a symphony of voices that spans the ages. The rediscovery of this language legacy became not only an academic success but also a cultural treasure in the modern world. It establishes a connection between the present and a linguistic past that was on the verge of being lost to the sands of time.

2.4 Protagonist deciphers initial symbols, hinting at a lost culture

In the midst of an archaeological expedition, against the backdrop of the silent ruins of Mohenjo-Daro, the protagonist, an intrepid archaeologist, sets out on a trip that will unveil the mysteries of a spoken language that has been lost to time. The protagonist, armed with perseverance and a keen eye, deciphers the initial symbols inscribed into ancient artifacts, opening a gateway to a vanished culture that has been buried behind the layers of time.

As the main character carefully removes the dust that has accumulated over the course of millennia from a seal that has been intricately etched, a feeling of expectation permeates the atmosphere. Under the meticulous study of the protagonist's trained eyes, the symbols, which were before enigmatic and incomprehensible, show signs of beginning to unveil their secrets. With each stroke and curve of the old script, a puzzle piece is created, and it is just ready to be inserted into the bigger mosaic of comprehension.

The initial breakthrough is not solely a result of language expertise; rather, it is the result of a profound appreciation for the contextual richness of the silent ruins. As someone who is well-versed in the art of archaeological interpretation, the protagonist makes use of the mutually beneficial relationship that exists between artifacts and the cultural environment in which they were found.

When evaluated in conjunction with the objects that surround the seal, the symbols on the seal begin to tell a tale. This story is a narrative of a culture that once flourished in the shadows of Mohenjo-Daro.

The symbols that have been deciphered provide evidence of a complex communication system, showing that the language in question is structured and has its own grammar and syntax. Using a feeling of historical empathy as a compass, the protagonist starts to recognize patterns and motifs that appear repeatedly throughout the screenplay. As a result of careful comparison and analysis, the linguistic puzzle begins to take shape, and the first symbols become the Rosetta Stone that unlocks the door to a lost world in terms of language.

An unfolding of a cultural panorama takes place while the protagonist works to interpret the symbols. It would appear that the script is entangled with a variety of actions, including religious acts, daily rituals, and possibly even administrative records. The symbols that are found on pottery fragments provide the impression that they are connected to business and commerce, whereas the symbols that are found on seals give the impression that they are depicting mythological figures or a social hierarchy. The main character, who is experiencing an increasing sense of wonder, comes to the realization that each symbol is not only essential to comprehending the language, but also the complexities of a civilization that was once so prosperous.

During this crucial juncture, the protagonist transforms into a conduit between the past and the present, bringing the lifeless ruins to life. A glimpse into the thoughts, expressions, and intellectual pursuits of a people who lived along the banks of the Indus River thousands of years ago can be gained through the deciphering of the symbols. During the course of the protagonist's laborious efforts, the latent culture that has been lost in the screenplay starts to start speaking.

The ramifications of this breakthrough in linguistics extend far beyond the world of academics. In addition to shedding light on the larger cultural history of the Indus Valley Civilization, the decipherment of the protagonist not only helps to the comprehension of a language that has been forgotten, but it also shines light there. The lost culture, which was previously obscured by the sands of time, becomes a tangible element of the narrative that is prevalent in the present day.

It is the news of the protagonist's breakthrough that reverberates throughout the scholarly community, and it is this news that sparks a renewed interest in the silent ruins of Mohenjo-Daro.

After then, collaborations with linguists, historians, and cultural specialists take place, which results in the creation of a multidisciplinary approach to further interpret the script and unravel the nuances of the civilization that has been lost. The first triumph of the protagonist serves as a catalyst for a broader project, which is a collaborative endeavor to put together the linguistic and cultural puzzle of a civilization that has been reduced to whispers in the wind for a very long time.

Throughout the course of the protagonist's quest to comprehend the initial symbols, the reverberation of a society that has been lost reverberates through the ages. After having been stoic in their mysteries for a long time, the silent ruins now beckon with a newfound life. The lost culture is reclaiming its place in the mosaic of human history as the protagonist continues to unravel the linguistic tapestry. This reclamation invites us to listen to the stories of the lost culture, consider the accomplishments of the lost culture, and recognize the continuing legacy of the lost culture.

Chapter 3

Echoes of a Forgotten Language

Echoes can be heard reverberating across the lonely ruins of Mohenjo-Daro and Harappa, where the winds carry the whispers of time. These echoes are a language that has been forgotten and is waiting to be rediscovered. In this investigation, we dig into the mysterious script that was etched into the relics of the Indus Valley Civilization. We trace the process of decipherment that reveals the linguistic and cultural legacy of a people that has been lost to the annals of history.

The Ruins That Are Not Visible as Witnesses:

Both Mohenjo-Daro and Harappa, which are considered to be the crown jewels of the ancient Indus Valley Civilization, are silent witnesses to a civilization that flourished along the banks of the powerful Indus River until the present day. In the middle of the ruins of granaries, bathhouses, and residential quarters, the script that is gracing seals, ceramics, and buildings beckons to those who are interested in deciphering the mysteries of a language that has been forgotten.

The motionless ruins give parts of a linguistic conundrum as archaeologists gently tread over the ancient streets. The script, which has not been deciphered, provides a hint at the intellectual and cultural wealth of a civilization that has been buried in the folds of time. The endeavor to decode these symbols turns into an adventure, a quest to bring the mutterings of a language that has been forgotten to life.

The mystery around the script:

Linguists have been unable to comprehend the script of the Indus Valley Civilization for a very long time, despite the fact that it is visually attractive. It consists of a collection of inscriptions, characters, and symbols that are used to decorate artifacts like pottery, seals, and other objects. The difficulty rests not only in the complicated intricacy of the symbols, but also in the absence of a linguistic Rosetta Stone, which would be a key that would bridge the ancient writing with a language that is already understood.

Researchers in the fields of linguistics, archaeology, and history have been fascinated by the script for many years.

The mystery surrounding its meaning has given rise to a great number of speculations, which in turn have sparked arguments and fueled a communal desire to decipher the language code that would expose the stories, thoughts, and expressions of the ancient inhabitants. Contemporary explorers are invited to decipher a language that has been dormant for millennia by taking use of the silent ruins that are studded with these mysterious markings.

The Odyssey of the Protagonist:

At the center of this intellectual endeavor is our protagonist, an archaeologist whose unyielding dedication to deciphering the language that has been forgotten is fueled by his enthusiasm for solving the mysteries of the past. The protagonist, armed with scholastic rigor and an insatiable curiosity, sets out on an adventure amid the lonely ruins of Mohenjo-Daro, where the first remnants of the language that has been forgotten are waiting for him.

The journey starts with the careful handling of ancient artifacts, such as seals that bear the script that was once used to seal goods and documents, pottery that is engraved with symbols that hint at the daily lives of the ancient people, and architectural elements that whisper stories of a civilization's cultural and spiritual tapestry. A voyage into the linguistic core of the Indus Valley Civilization begins when the protagonist, through careful observation and scholarly acumen, deciphers the earliest symbols. This marks the beginning of the adventure.

The interpretation of the context:

The decipherment of the protagonist is not merely the decoding of symbols; rather, it is a skill that involves the analysis of context. A contextual canvas is provided by the silent ruins, which are characterized by their stratigraphic layers and items that have been meticulously preserved. The protagonist uses this canvas to paint a linguistic tale. In the larger context of their archaeological surrounds, the symbols begin to reveal not only linguistic meanings but also cultural nuances. This is because the symbols are part of the archeological context.

The main character is able to recognize patterns of usage, which include symbols that are related with commercial transactions, religious rituals, and possibly administrative activities. It is through the lens of contextual interpretation that the script, which was once an abstract collection of characters, transforms into a living language. Every symbol that is deciphered brings us one step closer to comprehending the myriad of features that comprise a civilization that has been forgotten, and the ghostly ruins start to reverberate with the voices of a people who have been gone for a very long time.

The field of comparative linguistics: bringing together disparate threads over time

Comparative linguistics becomes an important tool for the protagonist as they continue to probe deeper into the decipherment.

The protagonist makes an effort to discover linguistic cognates and to decipher the linguistic family to which the ancient script may belong by establishing linkages between the symbols of the language that have been forgotten and those of known linguistic systems.

In order to complete the journey, it is necessary to navigate the linguistic tapestry of nearby regions, investigate relationships with languages spoken in contemporaneous civilizations, and identify shared linguistic foundations. The field of comparative linguistics functions as a connector between different eras, bringing together the various threads of linguistic development and developing tentative correlations that lead to a more comprehensive understanding of the language that has been forgotten.

A Rosetta Stone, Whether It Be Real or Metaphorical:

In order to decode the language that has been forgotten, the protagonist is on a mission to find a Rosetta Stone, which may be thought of as either an artifact or a metaphorical key that would serve as a point of reference regarding translation. In the process of deciphering the ancient script's linguistic code, the Rosetta Stone plays a crucial role, regardless of whether it is an actual artifact that has been inscribed or a comparative linguistic anchor.

The main character, who is propelled by the tantalizing promise of a breakthrough, examines inscriptions with a keen eye for detail. It is possible that a multilingual artifact may emerge, which will contain the forgotten script in addition to a language that is already recognized. This will provide a parallel that will allow for a more accurate decipherment. An important turning point in the protagonist's journey is the symbolic unlocking of the forgotten language by the use of a Rosetta Stone, regardless of whether the Rosetta Stone is genuine or figurative.

The Cultural Resonance of Stone and Symbols: Stories in Stone and Symbols

In addition to the linguistic complexities, the deciphering of the long-lost language reveals a cultural resonance that is inscribed in the symbols. The protagonist, who is now aware of the story that has been etched into stone and clay, sees symbols not just as linguistic units but also as bearers of cultural expressions, beliefs, and societal practices.

Not only do the symbols on seals depict abstract characters, but they also depict scenes from everyday life, figures representing mythology, and animals. Pottery that has been ornamented with the writing transforms into a canvas that reflects the creative preferences of the ancient culture who created it. When the stories of people who communicated not just through spoken words but also through the poetry of symbols are told, the ruins, which were once stoic and mysterious, become animated with the narrative.

The Obstacles to Decipherment: A Mystery That Remains Unsolved:

There are obstacles to overcome throughout the journey of the protagonist. In order to be successful in deciphering a language that has been forgotten, one must navigate a complex maze of unknowns, speculations, and occasionally dead ends. There is no live community that speaks the language, which makes things more complicated. As a result, the intricacies of pronunciation, idiomatic idioms, and contextual usage are cloaked in obscurity.

Within the academic community, there is the potential for controversies to emerge, with contrasting interpretations and conflicting scientific hypotheses. A strategy that draws from multiple disciplines is required in order to overcome the difficulties associated with decipherment. This technique encourages collaboration amongst linguists, historians, archaeologists, and cultural experts. An additional element of humility is added to the journey of the protagonist by the remaining mystery, which serves as a warning that some secrets from the past may continue to be elusive.

The Revealing: Reverberations That Do Not Disappear Through Time:

As the protagonist perseveres through the difficulties and uncertainties, a moment of revelation arrives. This is the point at which the language that has been lost begins to reveal its secrets. The script that has been decoded is transformed into a linguistic tapestry that reverberates with the voices of the old civilization. The previously mysterious ruins, which are now resonant with the linguistic cadence of a people who lived, loved, traded, and worshiped along the Indus River, have grown mute.

The unveiling is not only a success for the protagonist, but it is also a victory for humanity as a whole. It is a bridge that spans millennia, connecting contemporary researchers with the intellectual accomplishments of their ancient counterparts. Contemporary explorers are invited to listen, contemplate, and enjoy the linguistic and cultural legacy that arises from the silent ruins as the echoes of the language that has been forgotten continue to resound through time.

Bridging the Gap Between the Past and the Present: Contemporary Significance

In addition to extending its significance into the modern world, the deciphering of the language that has been forgotten surpasses the confines of the academic world. The heritage of the Indus Valley Civilization, both linguistically and culturally, serves as a bridge between the past and the present, encouraging a sense of continuity and interconnectedness.

In a world that places a greater emphasis on the preservation of cultural heritage, the rediscovery of a language that has been lost to time serves as a catalyst for cultural revival efforts. It is becoming increasingly important to prioritize educational programs, community engagement, and projects that aim to conserve and promote linguistic heritage.

A live witness to the perseverance of a civilization that has left an unmistakable impact on the collective memory of humanity, the echoes of the language that has been forgotten become a living testament on the subject.

The intrepid protagonist leads us on a trip of decipherment as we tour the silent ruins of Mohenjo-Daro and Harappa as part of the investigation of echoes from a language that has been forgotten. After being silent and incomprehensible for a long time, the ancient script is now transformed into a symphony of voices that reverberate through the historical corridors.

The linguistic odyssey, which is characterized by difficulties, disclosures, and the rediscovery of cultural traditions, extends an invitation to us to listen to the music that lingers in the winds of time. A monument that transcends the years and calls us to solve the mysteries, examine the stories, and commemorate the heritage of a civilization that whispered its secrets through symbols etched in stone, the echoes of the language that has been forgotten become a tribute to the persistence of human expression after it has been forgotten.

3.1 Dive into linguistic challenges faced by the protagonist

Where the echoes of an old script resound through the motionless ruins of Mohenjo-Daro, the protagonist starts on a tough quest that is loaded with problems. This adventure takes place in the labyrinthine world of linguistic decipherment. An odyssey that is distinguished by uncertainties, conflicts, and the relentless pursuit of linguistic comprehension is the effort to unravel the forgotten language of the Indus Valley Civilization. This search is a multifaceted odyssey. In this investigation, we delve into the complex web of difficulties that the protagonist must overcome in order to negotiate the linguistic maze that is hidden inside the mysterious symbols of a bygone era.

The Secretive Characteristics of the Script:

The opaque character of the screenplay itself contributes significantly to the difficulties that the protagonist is experiencing with language. An elaborate riddle is presented by the symbols, characters, and inscriptions that are found on the items that were produced by the Indus Valley Civilization. A linguistic Rosetta Stone, which would be a key to bridge the writing with a known language, is not available, which adds to the intricacy of the situation.

The narrative, while visually engaging and creatively presented, is something that is difficult to understand right away. In contrast to other ancient scripts that are more immediately recognizable, such as cuneiform or hieroglyphs, the symbols of the Indus script do not have any obvious phonetic or ideographic connotations. A script that has been resistant to linguistic deconstruction for generations is presented to the protagonist, who must undertake the challenging task of deciphering it.

The absence of a community that is still alive:

The process of deciphering a language becomes significantly more difficult when there is no living community that speaks that language. In contrast to languages that are spoken by people living in the present day, the language of the Indus Valley Civilization that has been forgotten does not have a linguistic community that can supply information on pronunciation, idiomatic expressions, and the development of language throughout time.

A degree of ambiguity is introduced into the situation because there is no living community present. There is still a lot of room for speculation regarding the intricacies of spoken language, the variances in regional dialects, and the contextual interpretation of words. It is necessary for the protagonist to face the difficulty of recreating a language that is devoid of the living voices that formerly animated its expressions.

Comparative Linguistics and the Limited Data Available for Comparison:

Comparative linguistics is an approach that seeks to establish connections between the language that has been forgotten and other linguistic systems that are already understood. The protagonist makes use of this tool. However, due to the small amount of comparable data that is currently accessible, this strategy is riddled with significant difficulties. Because it does not appear to have any obvious connections to other ancient languages, the Indus script is considered to be a linguistic anomaly.

The study of comparative linguistics is based on the identification of links between languages through the utilization of cognates, shared linguistic characteristics, and acoustic similarities. There are not many scripts that are comparable to the Indus script that were used by civilizations that were active at the same time, which presents a significant obstacle. To navigate the linguistic environment, the protagonist must rely on incomplete facts and supposition. There are few signposts to guide them across the landscape.

The presence of ambiguity in the representation of symbols:

The symbols of the Indus script, despite their outstanding visual appearance, provide a challenge when it comes to the portrayal of symbols graphically. Were the symbols primarily logographic, meaning that they represented words or concepts, or were they phonetic, meaning that they captured the sounds of a language that was spoken? The process of deciphering is made more difficult by the ambiguity that is present in symbolic representation.

At several points in the story, the protagonist comes across symbols that can have a variety of meanings or have different phonetic values. It is possible for a single sign to stand in for a whole thought, a single syllable, or even an entire phrase.

In order to decipher the script, one must not only possess linguistic expertise but also have a profound comprehension of the cultural setting in which the symbols were utilized.

The absence of a Rosetta Stone regarding language:

It might be possible to decipher the linguistic code with the help of a linguistic Rosetta Stone, which is a tangible item that has inscriptions in both the language that has been forgotten and a language that is already known. It is unfortunate that a Rosetta Stone of this kind for the Indus script has not yet been discovered. The deciphering effort is made more difficult by the fact that there is no corresponding inscription in a language that is already understood.

The protagonist is forced to rely on creative approaches, contextual cues, and interdisciplinary teamwork in order to deduce meanings and linguistic structures because there is no Rosetta Stone for language learning. In the course of the protagonist's journey, one of the most important challenges that they face is the search for a figurative Rosetta Stone.

Cultural Differences and the Obstacles Presented by Setting:

In addition to their significance in the language, the symbols of the Indus script have not just linguistic meanings but also cultural nuances and contextual connotations. In order for the protagonist to decipher the writing, it is necessary for them to not only comprehend the linguistic grammar, but also to interpret the symbols within the context of the larger cultural tapestry that is the Indus Valley Ancient Civilization.

In addition to being merely language utterances, the symbols that are found on artifacts such as seals, pottery, and other objects are loaded with extensive meanings. These can be depictions of situations from everyday life, narratives from mythology, or rites from religious practices. While the protagonist is making their way through the silent ruins, they are faced with the challenge of determining the cultural context in which the symbols were embedded.

Controversies and Competing Theories:

It is not uncommon for the deciphering of a language that has been forgotten to become a fruitful arena for scholarly debates and rival viewpoints. It is possible for linguists, archaeologists, and historians to come up with different interpretations of symbols, grammatical structures, and links across languages. During the course of the protagonist's search for clarity, they are required to navigate the academic environment, which is characterized by contrasting perspectives.

The legitimacy of the decipherment methods, the postulated language family of the script, and the overall dependability of the interpretations are all potential areas of contention that could bring about disagreements. Not only does the voyage of the protagonist become an odyssey of decipherment, but it also becomes a process of intellectual negotiation within the community of academics.

Unstable Linguistic Reconstructions:

When it comes to interpreting a language that has been forgotten, linguistic reconstructions, which are an essential component, are intrinsically unstable. The instability of reconstructions can be attributed to a number of factors, including the lack of a comprehensive linguistic corpus, the lack of clarity regarding phonetic values, and the fluid character of linguistic evolution throughout time.

It is necessary for the protagonist to deal with the fluidity of linguistic reconstructions when they are in the process of deciphering the sentence. Depending on the new evidence, the hypotheses that were given at one point in time may be updated or refined, which presents the protagonist with the challenge of remaining adaptable and open to developing interpretations.

The importance of interdisciplinary collaboration, as well as the difficulties it presents:

The deciphering of a language that has been lost to time requires the participation of professionals from a variety of fields, including linguists, archaeologists, historians, and cultural specialists. Despite the fact that teamwork is necessary for achieving a full knowledge, it also brings about its own unique set of difficulties. Various fields of study each bring their own distinct approaches, points of view, and preconceived notions to the table.

In order to successfully negotiate the intricacies of interdisciplinary collaboration, the protagonist is required to reconcile linguistic studies with archeological findings, historical settings, and cultural interpretations. Not only is it difficult to decipher the writing, but it is also difficult to weave together a whole story that takes into account the linguistic nuances that are present within the larger context of ancient society.

Protecting Cultural Sensitivity While Taking Ethical Considerations Into Account:

In the course of the protagonist's efforts to interpret a language that has been lost to history, he or she is confronted with ethical problems concerning the preservation of heritage and cultural sensitivity. The symbols of the Indus script, which are embedded in the relics of a civilization that was once prosperous, carry a profound cultural value for current populations that are tied to the region of the Indus Valley.

It is imperative that the protagonist approach the decipherment with a sense of reverence for the cultural inheritance that is embodied by the script. The difficulty lies in striking a balance between the academic quest of learning and the ethical responsibility to protect and honor the cultural heritage of the Indus Valley Civilization.

The adventure to decode the forgotten language of the Indus Valley Civilization unfolds as an elaborate tapestry of uncertainties and victories as the protagonist navigates the maze of linguistic hurdles that he or she must overcome. The fact that the script is mysterious, the fact that there is no live society, and the fact that comparative linguistics is complicated all add to the fact that this is a challenging journey.

However, the protagonist, who is driven by dogged determination and a strong academic acumen, delves deeply into the maze of language. The absence of a verbal Rosetta Stone, ambiguities in the depiction of symbols, and cultural nuances all become obstacles that must be surmounted. The process of deciphering the message is made more difficult by the presence of controversies, unstable reconstructions, and collaboration between different discipline groups.

During the course of the protagonist's journey through these obstacles, the endeavor transforms into not simply a scholastic undertaking but also a demonstration of the consistent human desire to acquire knowledge. A linguistic voyage that commemorates the past, explores the present, and affects the future understanding of a civilization's linguistic legacy is beckoned ahead by the echoes of the forgotten language, which, although being muffled by the sands of time, call the protagonist forward.

3.2 Introduction of a linguistic expert to aid in the decoding process

There is a pivotal moment that takes place in the dimly lit chambers of linguistic mystery, where the symbols of the Indus script dance like shadows on ancient artifacts. This moment is the introduction of a linguistic luminary, whose expertise becomes a beacon in the protagonist's quest to decode the forgotten language of the Indus Valley Civilization. Throughout the course of this story, we dig into the appearance of the linguistic specialist, a figure whose ideas, approaches, and scholastic prowess illuminate the road through the linguistic labyrinth. As a result, the protagonist is brought one step closer to deciphering the mysterious script.

The Force That Drives Workouts Together:

It is during this time that the protagonist is standing in the midst of the silent ruins, struggling with the difficulties of decipherment, that the appeal for collaboration is heard. It is at this point that a well-known linguist makes their entrance onto the stage. This is a person who is renowned for their contributions to the deciphering of ancient inscriptions and their multidisciplinary approach to solving linguistic issues.

The appearance of the linguistic luminary serves as a catalyst for the revitalization of newfound vigor and optimism. With the help of the linguistic expert's sophisticated understanding of ancient languages, the collaborative attempt is said to have the potential to bring together the insights that the protagonist has gained from the archeological domain. When they work together, they make a formidable pair that is ready to take on the complexities of the language that has been forgotten and to give the symbols that have been inscribed into the stones of Mohenjo-Daro a sense of life.

The credentials of the linguistic luminary are as follows:

Before the linguistic expert takes the stage, a quick examination of their credentials is conducted in order to set the stage for the key role that they will play in the decipherment tale once they arrive. An experienced linguist, the expert is well-versed in the complexities of decoding ancient writings and unraveling linguistic secrets that have baffled researchers for decades. He or she is considered to be an expert in the field.

The linguistic luminary not only brings a wealth of knowledge to the table, but they have also received praise for their prior efforts to the deciphering of other ancient languages. Their portfolio includes successful cooperation with archaeologists, historians, and cultural experts, which is a tribute to their capacity to bridge the gap between theoretical foundations of linguistics and practical applications in the field of archaeology.

Reputation in the Academic Community and Methodologies:

A long shadow is thrown over the terrain of linguistic studies as a result of the linguistic luminary's intellectual reputation, which precedes them. The approaches that they employ are not just founded on linguistic theory, but they are also reinforced by a thorough knowledge of the cultural and historical circumstances in which languages develop.

The competence of the expert extends over a wide variety of linguistic fields, including phonetics, syntax, semantics, and comparative linguistics, among others. The fact that they are able to negotiate the complexity of linguistic reconstructions, which is a key component of decoding forgotten languages, puts them as a guide through the linguistic nuances that have confused both academics and enthusiasts alike.

The Dynamics of Collaborative Work:

When the protagonist and the language expert decide to work together, the dynamics of collaboration become the focal point of the story. One of the defining characteristics of the relationship is the mutually beneficial exchange of information, approaches, and points of view.

It is the protagonist's knowledge with the artifacts and cultural nuances that contribute to the linguistic conversation, while the theoretical insights of the linguistic luminary find practical application in the setting of the archeological site.

The process of deciphering becomes propelled forward by the synergy that results from collective efforts. The capacity of the linguistic expert to convey intricate linguistic ideas to the protagonist, who might not be as well-versed in linguistic theory, helps to create an atmosphere in which there is a mutual understanding. Together, they set out on a trip that goes beyond the confines of their own fields of study, bringing together linguistic and archaeological threads in order to reveal the linguistic tapestry of the Indus Valley Civilization.

Deciphering Strategies: A Fresh Perspective on Ancient Symbols:

A new point of view on the decipherment tactics is brought about by the entrance of the linguistic expert. In order to provide the protagonist with an introduction to creative approaches, the expert draws inspiration from successful decipherment initiatives of other ancient inscriptions. During the process of deciphering, it is necessary to do comparative analyses with existing languages, recognize patterns, and have a detailed grasp of the evolution of language.

Within the framework of a language system, the linguistic luminary urges the protagonist to consider the symbols not just as immovable entities but also as aspects that are always evolving. The ability of the expert to recognize language patterns, recognize themes that appear repeatedly, and extract probable phonetic values from the symbols gives the decoding endeavor a fresh lease on life.

In the search for linguistic cognates, the process of tracing ancestral roots

The search for linguistic cognates, which are shared linguistic traits, phonetic similarities, and structural parallels that may relate the forgotten language to known linguistic systems, is one of the most important contributions that the linguistic expert makes. The linguistic luminary navigates the broad territory of language evolution in order to trace ancestral roots, drawing on the skills of comparative linguistics in the process.

The process of deciphering becomes significantly more important when it comes to the search for linguistic cognates. A specialist in linguistics, equipped with a complete understanding of language families and historical linguistic linkages, investigates the possibility of connections between the symbols of the Indus script and languages that were spoken in surrounding locations during the same historical period.

Contextual Insights: Untangling the Cultural Threads:

The linguistic expert highlights the significance of contextual insights in the process of interpreting the language that has been forgotten, building on the collaborative dynamics that have been established. When evaluated within the larger framework of archeological discoveries, cultural behaviors, and religious beliefs, the symbols begin to disclose not only language meanings but also cultural nuances. This is because the symbols are a consequence of the larger context.

An additional layer of complexity is added to the deciphering process by the linguistic luminary's ability to disentangle the cultural strands that are weaved within the script. The expert evaluates the inscriptions in light of the conceivable roles that they could play in administrative records, religious ceremonies, or daily communications as they lead the protagonist through the maze of symbols. As the pieces of the contextual puzzle begin to fall into place, the linguistic tapestry, which was previously veiled, becomes more clear.

Theoretical Frameworks and Linguistic Reconstructions:

During the process of deciphering, the linguistic expert will present theoretical frameworks that will guide the procedure. With the help of well-established language theories, the illuminator develops ideas for the phonetic values, grammatical structures, and semantic meanings that are encoded in the symbols. Theoretical frameworks serve as the scaffolding upon which language reconstructions are constructed.

The protagonist, with the assistance of the linguistic specialist, undertakes the laborious work of reconstructing the language in question. The unstable character of reconstructions, which was a challenge that the protagonist alone had to face, becomes a task that the protagonist and the linguistic luminary work together to overcome. Through the joint efforts of these individuals, linguistic hypotheses are refined, which ultimately results in a more detailed understanding of the grammar and syntax of the forgotten language.

The Rosetta Stone of Linguistic Translation: A Conceptualization of the Theory:

The concept is presented by the linguistic expert as a theoretical construction, a metaphorical key that bridges the ancient script with a language that is already understood. This is because there is no actual Rosetta Stone in the field of linguistics. A comparison anchor for linguistic analysis is provided by this conceptual Rosetta Stone, which becomes a focal point in the process of deciphering the language.

Through the assistance of the linguistic luminary, the protagonist is able to determine the possible linguistic connections that exist between the symbols of the Indus script and the languages that are currently in use.

The theoretical passages that juxtapose the language that has been forgotten with a linguistic relative become reference points, which help in the deciphering of inscriptions and symbols that had been a mystery up until this point.

Ethical Considerations and Cultural Sensitivity and Considerations:

The linguistic expert adds a nuanced perspective to the ethical considerations that are inherent in the process as the process of deciphering the language proceeds. It is now widely acknowledged that the symbols, which were long considered to be linguistic entities, are transmitters of cultural legacy. The luminary of the field of linguistics highlights the significance of treating the decipherment with cultural sensitivity, recognizing the great meaning of the symbols to modern populations that are tied to the location of the Indus Valley.

Because the protagonist and the language specialist are attempting to strike a delicate balance between academic research and cultural preservation, the united effort takes on an ethical dimension. In addition to contributing to a more comprehensive comprehension of the Indus Valley Civilization, the advice provided by the linguistic luminary guarantees that the process of deciphering the script ensures that the cultural history that is embedded in the script is respected.

The introduction of a linguistic luminary emerges as a transformative chapter in the ongoing story of deciphering the forgotten language of the Indus Valley Civilization. This brings about a significant change in the narrative. A symphony of interdisciplinary discoveries is created as a result of the partnership between the linguistic expert and the protagonist. This collaboration weaves together language theories, archaeological results, and cultural nuances.

The luminaries of linguistics, with their academic credentials, new approaches, and spirit of collaboration, sheds light on the shadows that are cast by the mysterious symbols of the Indus script. Confronting problems with perseverance and breathing life into the silent echoes of a language that has been forgotten, they explore the linguistic labyrinth together with the protagonist.

The cooperation between the linguistic luminary and the protagonist shows the power of collaboration in the process of unveiling ancient mysteries as the process of decoding the language progresses. In the process of dissipating the shadows of language ambiguity, a linguistic tapestry is revealed. This tapestry connects the modern world with the enduring legacy of the Indus Valley Civilization. It is a tribute to the transformational effect of expertise, collaboration, and the shared quest of knowledge.

3.3 Discovery of inscriptions that provide glimpses into daily life and rituals

The excavation of inscriptions that offer tantalizing views into the everyday life and customs of a civilization that has been lost to the sands of time is a significant discovery that is unfolding in the hushed corridors of time, where the ancient echoes of the Indus Valley Civilization continue to linger. The silent ruins of Mohenjo-Daro and Harappa begin to speak through the symbols and characters etched onto seals, pottery, and artifacts as researchers carefully sweep away the layers of history. This is happening throughout the course of the excavation process. For the purpose of providing a glimpse into the vivid tapestry of ordinary life and religious ceremonies that existed within the mysterious realm of the Indus Valley Civilization, this narrative investigates the significant finding of inscriptions.

The Ruins That Are Remaining Silent:

When the voyage starts, it is in the midst of the quiet ruins of Mohenjo-Daro and Harappa, where the remnants of an old civilization lie dormant, waiting to be revealed. While archaeologists are painstakingly excavating the vestiges of granaries, dwelling quarters, and public structures, their attention shifts to the inscriptions that are dispersed over the items. As the investigation progresses, the symbols, which were before mysterious and cryptic, become the focal object of attention. They have the capacity to reveal the mysteries of daily life and practice.

When it comes to understanding, seals serve as gateways

Seals, which are among the artifacts that produce inscriptions, stand out as particularly significant gates to understanding the rituals and daily life of the civilization that flourished in the Indus Valley. These seals, which were frequently artistically carved with symbols and characters, served a dual purpose: they served to seal goods and documents, and they also functioned as a canvas for artistic and linguistic expression.

Archaeologists are uncovering seals from a wide variety of situations, which has led to the discovery of a significant number of symbols. Not only do the inscriptions on these seals constitute a linguistic conundrum, but they also invite academics to interpret not only the grammatical complexities of the script, but also the cultural and ritualistic connotations that are embedded within them.

Deciphering the Daily Chronicles: the Third Section

Upon deciphering the inscriptions, the everyday records of the civilization that flourished in the Indus Valley revealed themselves. Scenes of lively marketplaces, commercial transactions, and agricultural operations are shown by the symbols that are etched into seals. Through the lens of language, the protagonists of daily life, such as merchants, farmers, and artisans, are brought to life, providing a vivid picture of the economic vitality and social connections of civilization.

The writings that are seen on seals function like old receipts, identifying transactions and showing ownership. Through the process of deciphering the symbols, the economic systems, trade networks, and market dynamics that were characteristic of everyday life are revealed. Words that are associated with items, measurements, and trading relationships come into being, which give light on the complex economic infrastructure that was responsible for maintaining the civilization.

Pottery Narratives: Symbols of Everyday Life in the Pottery Industry

In addition to being used as seals, pottery was also used as a canvas for the inscriptions that described the routine activities of the people who lived in the Indus Valley. There is a mosaic of daily activities, domestic sceneries, and culinary traditions that can be found on fragments of pottery that have been decorated with symbols. By deciphering the script that is written on pottery, a linguistic guide is created, which reveals the stories that are concealed within the vessels.

It is possible that the markings on pottery convey preferences in the realm of cuisine, implying the kinds of foods that are consumed and possibly the culinary rites that are related with meetings of a community. The scenes of domestic life that emerge are images of families participating in a variety of activities, which provide insight into the roles and relationships that exist inside the family. Not only do the inscriptions on ceramic fragments become linguistic artifacts, but they also become windows into the personal elements of everyday life.

Sacred Insights Can Be Unlocked Through the Use of Ritualistic Symbolism

Archaeologists are uncovering a spiritual dimension as they probe further into the inscriptions. This sacred dimension is the ritualistic meaning that is embedded within the script. A look into the spiritual fabric of the civilization can be gained through the interpretation of objects and seals that exhibit symbols linked with religious practices. The inscriptions that have been deciphered are the keys to comprehending the rituals, rites, and possibly even the pantheon of deities that the ancient people of the Indus Valley venerated.

Emerging from the shadows of language are symbols that are associated with fertility rites, worship, and ceremonial processions. The deciphering of these inscriptions will allow for the opening of a gateway to the holy places where the ancient people had their conversations with the divine. After having been mute witnesses to religious ceremonies in the past, the inscriptions on seals have now become the script of spiritual narratives that are ready to be received.

Contextual interpretation: combining linguistics and archaeology:

It is necessary to use a nuanced approach that integrates linguistic understanding with archeological context in order to decode inscriptions.

When symbols are interpreted within the larger framework of cultural and historical settings, the collaboration between linguists and archaeologists becomes increasingly important.

The interpretation of context becomes an art form, comprising a delicate dance between the meanings of symbols and the meanings of language in the context of the circumstance. The inscriptions on seals that are discovered in close proximity to particular structures or artifacts take on a greater relevance, providing clues about the purpose and function of the seals within the context of the everyday and ceremonial life of the culture for which they were discovered.

Unlocking Comprehensive Narratives Through Multidisciplinary Collaboration

Linguists, archaeologists, historians, and cultural experts are brought together as a result of the discovery of inscriptions, which sets off a surge of collaboration across multiple disciplines. The objective of the collaborative endeavor is not only to decrypt the linguistic code, but also to weave together comprehensive narratives that cover a wide range of behaviors and rituals that are performed on a daily basis.

Linguists give their experience in interpreting grammatical structures and linguistic nuances, archaeologists provide insights into the archaeological environment, and cultural experts contribute their grasp of the symbolic meanings embedded within the inscriptions. Linguists, archaeologists, and cultural experts all contribute to its interpretation. As a result of the partnership, a tapestry of information is created, which contributes to a deeper comprehension of the cultural and social fabric of the Indus Valley Civilization.

Expressions of Artistic Expression in Language: The Aesthetics of Symbols:

The aesthetics of symbols as creative expressions are revealed by the inscriptions that are found on seals and ceramics, in addition to the linguistic and cultural meaning of these symbols. The script, with its meticulously constructed characters and elaborate drawings, transforms into a type of visual communication that goes beyond the just functional. The elegance of the symbols gives the impression that there is a respect for artistic expression within the sphere of language.

Not only does the process of deciphering involve decoding the meanings of the many languages, but it also requires an appreciation for the artistic nuances that are inherent in the symbols. After having been seen as solely functional in the past, the inscriptions now take on an aesthetic dimension, exposing the artistic sensitivities of a culture that woven beauty into the fabric of its everyday and ritualistic existence.

The Revealing of Socioeconomic Structures: Hierarchies and Relationships

Inscriptions, in addition to providing insights into daily life, also reveal the socioeconomic institutions that served as the foundation for the civilization. The symbols that have been decoded provide insights into the social structures, occupations, and relationships that exist within the framework of those societies. As a result of the emergence of words linked with leadership, trade roles, and familial ties, academics are able to trace the complex network of social institutions.

The investigation of language goes beyond the immediate visual symbols and encompasses the subtle nuances that express the complexities of social relationships. The inscriptions that are found on seals that belong to various persons or groups provide evidence of ownership patterns, which may demonstrate the existence of familial or clan systems. The process of deciphering becomes an investigation into sociolinguistics, which helps to unravel the social fabric of the civilization that flourished in the Indus Valley.

A Discussion on Contemporary Reflections and the Continuity of Culture:

During the process of deciphering the inscriptions and bringing the narratives of daily life and rituals into light, the echoes of the Indus Valley Civilization reverberate with current perspectives. By preserving the language legacy through the symbols that are etched onto seals and ceramics, the linguistic legacy creates a bridge that connects the past with the present.

When current societies discover echoes of their historical past in the inscriptions that have been decoded, cultural continuity is shown to have been acknowledged. A celebration of cultural resilience, a monument to the enduring legacy of a civilization that whispered its stories via symbols engraved in stone, the linguistic analysis of daily life and rituals becomes not only an academic undertaking but also a celebration of cultural resilience.

During the course of the story of the Indus Valley Civilization, the discovery of inscriptions becomes a significant chapter. It is a trip into the linguistic tapestry that weaves together the everyday rhythms and religious rites of ancient people. Previously silent, the symbols now reverberate with tales of sacred ceremonies, kitchens, and marketplaces because of their significance. The translated inscriptions act as linguistic time capsules, providing a profound connection to the past and a look into the complex lives of those who walked the ancient streets of Mohenjo-Daro and Harappa. These writings were discovered over the course of several centuries. As archaeologists and linguists continue to find and translate these inscriptions, the echoes of the past continue to resound, beckoning modern explorers to listen, reflect, and commemorate the ongoing legacy of the civilization that flourished in the Indus Valley.

3.4 Clues suggesting a connection between the civilization and extraterrestrial beings

Certain mysteries in the fabric of human history defy the conventional answers that have been offered, which has led to theories that go beyond the confines of the realms that are based on earth. As a result of its enigmatic symbols, sophisticated cultural practices, and extensive urban design, the Indus Valley Civilization has become a canvas for investigation and speculation. Some of the numerous hypotheses propose that there is a tantalizing connection between this ancient society and extraterrestrial beings with whom it was associated. In contrast to the way that the majority of academic research tends to concentrate on terrestrial explanations, a fringe investigation of indications suggests that the ancient Indus landscape may have been intertwined with a cosmic tale.

Innovations in Technology and the Alignment of Astronomical Objects:

There is a thread that runs across the remarkable technological accomplishments of the Indus Valley Civilization, which is a part of the extraterrestrial theory. As potential indicators of influence beyond the capability of humans at the time, proponents point to the exceptional urban planning, the precision in architectural arrangement, and the complex drainage systems. In addition to adding gasoline to the fire of extraterrestrial hypothesis, the alignments of certain constructions with celestial bodies, such as the sun or particular stars, raise the possibility of an understanding of astronomy that extends beyond the realm of earthly astronomy.

The elaborate city plans, which include streets that are aligned to the cardinal directions, as well as the construction of complex structures such as the Great Bath at Mohenjo-Daro, feed arguments regarding the origin of such knowledge. What are the chances that the architects of the ancient cities were able to receive advice from alien entities, which would have provided them with great technological insights and astronomical knowledge?

Is There a Cosmic Language Behind Cryptic Symbols?

A further layer of complexity is added to the story of alien beings by the symbols of the Indus script, which are still generally difficult to comprehend. The proponents of this concept believe that the symbols might not be the result of human linguistic evolution but rather a cosmic language that was transmitted by extraterrestrial entities. Images that are reminiscent of descriptions linked with extraterrestrial encounters in more contemporary situations are evoked by the detailed carvings that are found on seals and artifacts. These sculptures resemble entities that have elongated heads or odd features.

The script that has not been deciphered is transformed into a cosmic code, which has the ability to reveal the mysteries of contact with extraterrestrial beings.

According to this belief, the elaborate patterns and symbols may have been an attempt by the ancient residents to record contacts with beings from beyond the stars or to transmit signals to alien entities. This theory was proposed by the ancient inhabitants.

Strange Representations and Unusual Occurrences:

Those who are interested in extraterrestrial life frequently draw attention to strange depictions that can be found in artifacts. These depictions point to a divergence from the typical depictions of human figures or animals. Some people believe that certain seals and sculptures portray humanoid figures wearing garb that resembles spacesuits or helmets. Others disagree with this interpretation. When seen through the prism of extraterrestrial conjecture, these peculiar representations transform into enticing evidence that hint at contacts with beings emanating from other worlds.

Furthermore, images of unusual machines or flying objects in ancient art have been regarded as evidence of advanced technology that was beyond the comprehension of the time period it was created. It's possible that these are creative representations of collisions with extraterrestrial spaceships or technologically advanced machines.

Unaccounted-for disappearances: had they departed from this planet?

There is a tangential part of the extraterrestrial idea that pertains to the Indus Valley Civilization that touches on the strange collapse and disappearance of the civilization itself. Some people believe that the reduction is due to a larger cosmic departure, while others believe that natural factors, changes in river routes, or internal socio-political difficulties are to blame for the declining population.

Is it possible that the unexpected abandonment of cities such as Mohenjo-Daro may be attributed to a celestial event or the departure of alien mentors who had directed the civilization? Due to the absence of clear evidence concerning the demise of the civilization, speculative narratives that contain the involvement of alien beings are presented as a viable option.

Intertwining Myth and Reality:

Most of the time, references to gods or other heavenly entities coming down from the skies may be found in ancient myths and religious literature from a variety of different religious traditions. In the backdrop of the civilization that flourished in the Indus Valley, there are enthusiasts who believe that the gods that the ancient people worshiped could have been extraterrestrial beings. It is possible that the complicated narratives found in religious writings could be regarded as encounters with beings from other realms, with technological marvels and divine traits that are beyond the comprehension of human beings.

Skepticism and the Search for Alternative Explanations:

In the larger realm of archaeology and history, the alien idea about the Indus Valley Civilization is still considered to be a fringe perspective. This is an important point to keep in mind. The necessity for theories that are supported by facts and have their origins in earthly environments is emphasized by mainstream academics. Skeptics contend that the advanced urban planning, symbolism, and oddities may be comprehended by putting them in the context of human inventiveness, the development of culture, and the intricacies of ancient societies.

As we make our way through the historical maze that is the Indus Valley Civilization, the extraterrestrial idea adds a layer of mystery and speculation to the situation. Although there are a few hints that might give the impression that there is a connection to the cosmos, the vast majority of academics stress the significance of grounded interpretations that are supported by facts. There is a possibility that the symbols, complex technology, and depictions found in artifacts hold the secrets to comprehending the inventiveness of an ancient culture rather than pointing to the intervention of those from another world.

In the end, the investigation of these hints will continue to be an intellectual voyage, a cosmic expedition through the halls of human history. The quest for understanding is an ongoing journey that goes beyond the earthly and reaches for the stars in the never-ending search for the mysteries of our past. Whether the Indus Valley Civilization bears the imprint of extraterrestrial influence or stands as a testament to human creativity and resilience, the journey continues.

Chapter 4

The Lost Archives

Throughout the enormous span of human history, there are epochs that have been hidden by the mists of time, leaving us with tantalizing gaps in our understanding of the periods that have passed. The idea of lost archives conjures up thoughts of secret troves of information, manuscripts that have been secreted, and wisdom that has been forgotten and is patiently waiting to be recovered. This story takes the reader on a journey through the halls of history, investigating the concept of lost archives and the deep consequences that they carry for the process of uncovering the mysteries that have been concealed in the shadows of time.

The Mystery of the Lost Archives:

A collection of documents, texts, or artifacts that have, for a variety of causes, faded away from the collective memory of humanity is referred to as "lost archives," and the word "lost archives" conjures a sense of curiosity. There are holes in our historical narrative that are represented by these archives, which are veiled in mystery. As a result, historians, enthusiasts, and academics are left to hypothesize about the vast amount of information that may be lying dormant and waiting to be discovered.

It is possible that these missing archives include ancient libraries that have been destroyed by time and conflict, as well as secret stores that have been purposefully concealed for reasons that are unknown. The fascination of lost archives comes in the potential treasures that they may contain. These treasures may include forgotten wisdom, stories that have not been recounted before, and a greater understanding of cultures and civilizations that have been lost during the course of history.

On the other hand, the Alexandria Library is a symbol of loss

The Library of Alexandria, which served as a light of knowledge in the ancient world, is often considered to be one of the most prominent representations of stolen archives. The library was established in the third century BCE, and it was a hub for intellectual interaction since it had a vast collection of scrolls, manuscripts, and books from a variety of cultures. The fate of the library, on the other hand, is a terrible narrative of destruction, since it has been destroyed by a number of different catastrophes over the course of several centuries, including fire, conflict, and neglect.

The destruction of the Library of Alexandria serves as a striking illustration of the extent to which large stores of information can be lost from the collective consciousness of humans. Because the scrolls that once contained the knowledge of experts from a variety of cultures are now echoed in the annals of history, contemporary scholars are left to conjecture about the intellectual treasures that were destroyed by the flames.

Ancient Libraries That Have Been Hidden:

There are further stories of hidden or lost archives that can be found throughout antiquity that go beyond the Library of Alexandria. For example, the Maya Codices were considered to be sacred scriptures by the Maya civilization. These codices contained important information such as astronomical observations, religious ceremonies, and cultural knowledge. Due to the fact that the majority of these codices were destroyed during the Spanish conquest, there are just a few fragments that can attest to the extent of the Maya's intellectual accomplishments.

In a similar manner, the ancient city of Herculaneum, which was buried by the eruption of Mount Vesuvius in the year 79 CE, is home to the mansion of the Papyri, which is a sumptuous Roman mansion that houses a vast library. Despite the fact that just a portion of the villa has been excavated, it is believed to contain intellectual works, possibly even works of Epicurean philosophy that have been lost. The buried scrolls, which were carbonized as a result of the volcanic explosion, continue to be a tantalizing mystery, waiting for technological developments that might eventually reveal their secrets.

Vanishing civilizations and silent archives:

The loss of a whole civilization's archives frequently occurs at the same time as the extinction of the civilization itself. When it comes to the fate of its written records, the mysterious Indus Valley Civilization, which is famous for its sophisticated urban planning and strange script, offers some intriguing possibilities. It is possible that the script that has not been deciphered appears on items and seals, and that this script holds the secrets to comprehending the daily lives, rituals, and governance of this ancient civilization. As a result of the silence of the Indus script, the lost archives have been given an additional degree of mystery, which has led to speculation regarding the information that is concealed inside its cryptic symbols.

The Olmecs, who were the ancestors of the Maya, were a Mesoamerican culture that left behind giant heads and beautiful carvings, but they did not have a known writing system. Due to the lack of written documents, there is a gap in our comprehension of their language, culture, and the structure of their society. For archaeologists and historians, the lost archives of ancient civilizations that have since gone continue to be a source of both intrigue and frustration.

The difficulty of deciphering the meaning of the phrase "lost in translation"

The endeavor to retrieve lost archives is confronted with the daunting obstacle of decipherment. Scripts that have not been deciphered, such as the Linear A alphabet used by the Minoans or the Etruscan language used in ancient Italy, are examples of linguistic mysteries that are difficult to comprehend. One of the most remarkable achievements in the history of understanding ancient Egyptian hieroglyphs is the discovery of the Rosetta Stone, which is a key to deciphering ancient Egyptian hieroglyphs.

Scholars are captivated by the possibility of discovering long-lost languages, histories, and cultural nuances contained inside the archives that have been lost and written in scripts that have not been deciphered. Not only is it difficult to read the symbols, but it is also difficult to piece together the larger context, which includes the cultural tapestry, historical events, and society systems that are recorded in these ancient texts.

The Deception Regarding the Secret Archives:

Beyond the historical examples of archives that have been misplaced, the idea of secret archives captivates the imagination with thoughts of secret repositories that are responsible for protecting information that is not widely known. The narratives of secret organizations, mystical texts, and esoteric wisdom that are protected in underground rooms are frequently woven together in the narratives of legends and conspiracy theories.

There is a repository that is supposed to store ancient texts, artifacts, and knowledge that is considered to be too delicate for public consumption. One example of such a legendary repository is the Vatican Secret Archives. The idea that there is a hidden archive that contains esoteric or prohibited knowledge is still a matter of speculation, despite the fact that the Vatican Archives are a legitimate institution that houses a massive collection of historical records. The combination of history, mystery, and the human obsession with the unknown is what gives secret archives their undeniable appeal.

Technological Resurrections: Digital Archives and Beyond for the Future:

At this point in time, technology has evolved into a tool that can be used for both the preservation of archives and the discovery of them. When it comes to the preservation of human history, digital archives, which are knowledge warehouses that can be accessed with the click of a mouse, offer a new frontier. The digitization of manuscripts, ancient writings, and historical documents is being carried out by institutions and organizations all around the world. This is being done to ensure that the information contained within these materials is not limited by the restrictions of physical degradation.

New opportunities have arisen as a result of developments in imaging technology, artificial intelligence, and computational linguistics, which have made it possible to read ancient scripts and rebuild manuscripts that have been destroyed or faded. There are new opportunities for researchers to investigate the depths of human history with a level of clarity that has never been seen before because of the possibility of technologically resurrecting vanished archives.

The legacy of the archives that were lost:

In addition to being an intellectual endeavor, the investigation of lost archives is also a search to reestablish a connection with the past and gain an understanding of the threads that are used to weave the fabric of human civilization. The legacy of vanished archives extends beyond the confines of academic institutions, having an impact on cultural narratives, serving as a source of inspiration for artistic creations, and molding the communal consciousness.

The idea of lost archives is frequently used as a source of inspiration in the fields of literature, art, and film. "The Name of the Rose" by Umberto Eco and "The Library of Babel" by Jorge Luis Borges are two examples of imaginative works that investigate the mystical appeal of concealed knowledge and the implications of its revelation. Throughout the history of cinema, audiences have been captivated by stories that revolve around ancient texts, hidden organizations, and lost civilizations. These stories are a reflection of the everlasting obsession with the unknown.

Ethical Considerations That Should Be Taken Into Account with Regard to Exploration:

In situations where the rediscovered knowledge is connected with the cultural and spiritual history of modern societies, the research of lost archives presents ethical problems. This is especially true in situations where the lost archives have been abandoned. When it comes to the deciphering of sacred texts, for instance, it is necessary to strike a delicate balance between academic research and respect for the beliefs and practices of those who hold these texts in high regard.

When it comes to the search for lost archives, cultural sensitivity becomes of the utmost importance. This is done to ensure that the pursuit of knowledge does not violate the cultural rights and identities of groups that are related to historical artifacts in the current day. The ethical considerations involved in exploration highlight the obligation that scholars and researchers have to approach lost archives with humility, recognizing the living legacies that are embedded in old wisdom.

Lost archives are a concept that attracts dreamers, academics, and explorers to explore the shadows and uncover the mysteries of the past. This concept is found within the labyrinth of history.

Stories of lost libraries, civilizations that have vanished, and scripts that have not been decoded compel us to embark on a search for knowledge that is not limited by the constraints of current time.

The hunt of lost archives is a demonstration of the continuing human curiosity that tries to shed light on the shadows that have been cast by the veils of time. These archives are gateways to understanding the complexity of human history, whether they are concealed in the ruins of ancient civilizations, buried behind layers of volcanic ash, or inscribed in characters that have not been deciphered.

Despite the fact that technology is always advancing and inter-disciplinary collaboration is flourishing, the process of recovering lost archives is still ongoing. It is possible that the shadows that have been surrounding these archives will eventually give way to the light of discovery, revealing information that has been hidden away for generations. We are about to go on a journey that transcends disciplines, across cultural borders, and invites us to see the echoes of our shared human heritage. This journey begins with our acceptance of the complexity of lost archives.

4.1 Protagonist stumbles upon hidden chambers with well-preserved scrolls

Our protagonist sets off on an archeological expedition that goes beyond the confines of history. This voyage takes place in the center of an ancient city, where time weaves its tapestry through forgotten lanes and silent ruins. During the dark light of discovery, the protagonist comes upon hidden rooms that have been hidden from the view of the world for a considerable amount of time. A gateway to unravel mysteries, decipher ancient knowledge, and unearth the stories that have been concealed beneath the folds of antiquity can be found within these hallowed sanctuaries, where well-preserved scrolls that have not been touched by the hands of time are waiting to be discovered.

The Odyssey of Archaeological Discovery:

In the beginning of the journey, the protagonist is an adventurous archaeologist who has a strong desire to untangle the mysterious threads that have been woven throughout history. The archaeologist heads into the heart of an old city that is soaked in the echoes of lost civilizations. Equipped with a trowel, a lamp, and a passion for discovery, the archaeologist sets out on his journey. It is the tempting promise of unknown secrets that drives them as they travel convoluted corridors and forgotten rooms. The whispers of history guide their footsteps as they make their way through these passages.

The Mysterious City and the Rumors That It Spreads:

An aura of mysticism appears to emanate from the old city, which may be a vestige of the civilization that flourished in the Indus Valley or a vanished metropolis from another era. Crumbling walls that are covered with symbols that cannot be read and carvings that have corroded convey stories of a time that has passed. The main character, who is sensitive to the language of stones and symbols, follows the trail of clues that take them further into the heart of the city, which is a place where shadows conceal secrets and time has left its stamp on every surface.

The Unexpected Occurrence of Events:

When it comes to archaeological activities, serendipity frequently lurks in the shadows, and our protagonist is well-versed in the unpredictability of this phenomenon. They are walking down a corridor that appears to be completely normal when they become aware of a slight draft or a change in the mood of the air. The protagonist arrives at the conclusion that there is more to the wall than initially appears to be the case by utilizing both the intuition of a scholar and the instinct of an adventurer. They have been invited to uncover the wonders that lay beyond a hidden door that has been carefully covered by the passage of time.

The Unveiling: A Chamber Steeped in Time:

A room that appears to be frozen in time materializes in front of the protagonist's eyes as the previously concealed entrance submits to the delicate touch of the protagonist's fingers. Within, the air is calm, and it is carrying the weight of the years around it. A space that has been uninhabited for millennia is entered by the archaeologist, and the flickering light of the lantern causes dust particles to dance around in the space. The walls, which are covered in murals that have faded over time, are a testament to scenes depicting daily life, ceremonies, and the splendor of a civilization.

An altar, representing what appears to be an offering to the gods of archaeology, can be seen at the very center of the room. The protagonist is not captivated by the sight of wealth or jewels; rather, it is the sight of ancient scrolls that are carefully organized on stone shelves that captures his attention. Something dawns on me: here is a secret storehouse, a library that has been lost to the passage of time.

The Scrolls: Keepers of Lost Knowledge and Knowledge Lost:

As they wait to be reawakened, the scrolls, which have been meticulously preserved in the cold and dry embrace of the room, are waiting. As the protagonist approaches the shelves, he or she is overcome with a mixture of reverence and exhilaration. Each scroll is a keeper of wisdom that has been lost to time, a messenger from a period of time that history has almost completely forgotten.

The materiality of the scrolls, which include the texture of ancient paper and the ink that has endured the test of time, is a testament to the tenacity of human endeavors to record and preserve information.

Script that has not been deciphered: deciphering the unreadable language

When the protagonist is searching through the scrolls, he comes across a linguistic conundrum known as the writing, which has been a mystery to academics for decades. The markings that have not been understood, which are delicately woven across the surfaces of the scrolls, reveal stories of a language that has been forgotten. In this same situation, the protagonist is presented with a challenge that piques his academic curiosity. They go on the voyage of decipherment, which is a mission to breathe life into the silent whispers of an old language, armed with linguistic prowess and a drive to figure out how to unlock the code.

The Revealing of Everyday Activities and Rituals:

During the process of the protagonist deciphering the script, the scrolls start to disclose the everyday rhythms and religious rites of the civilization that handed its legacy to these pages. The ebb and flow of daily life, as well as descriptions of bustling marketplaces and agricultural methods, are all presented in a manner that is elegantly written. A society that was administered by unseen hands is described in the scrolls. This society was characterized by religious harmony, communal harmony, and government that were all intertwined into the fabric of existence.

The protagonist is able to view the old city in its prime through the words that are written on the scrolls. He sees streets that are bustling with the chatter of merchants, temples that resound with the buzz of ceremonies, and common areas that are where the various strands of the civilization connect.

Recollections of Heroes and Legends That Have Been Lost:

Forgotten heroes and long-lost tales are brought back to life through the scrolls, which transcend the commonplace. Names that have been hidden by the sands of time are encountered by the protagonist. These names include leaders who directed their people through epochs, poets whose songs resonated through the centuries, and artists whose hands produced marvels that would endure in memory over the course of time. The scrolls serve as a connection between the modern world and the glorious past of a civilization, bridging the gap between the present and the reminders of the glory that once existed in the past.

The Observations of the Astronomer: Chronicles of the Heavens:

A single scroll stands out among the others; it is a chronicle written by an astronomer and it is a celestial map that has been engraved onto parchment.

The protagonist, who is mesmerized by the cosmic ballet that is detailed in minute detail, comes to the realization that this is more than just a chronological record of astronomical observations. In addition to being a guide to the stars, it is a demonstration of the civilization's profound comprehension of the universe.

The astronomer's scrolls contain information about a variety of topics, including eclipses, phases of the moon, and the motions of the planets. As the protagonist gazes at the same celestial bodies that once entered the ancients, he or she transforms into a time traveler by use of the common language of the stars.

The Stewards of Ancient Knowledge: Ethical Challenges and Consequences

The protagonist is faced with moral conundrums as a result of the discovery of the concealed chambers and the scrolls that have been preserved over time. They carry a tremendous burden on their shoulders as a result of the obligation of being a steward of ancient wisdom. There is a reverberation of questions regarding preservation, conservation, and accessibility that can be heard throughout the consciousness of the protagonist. In order to maintain the respectability of the discovery, how much information should be made available to the general public, and how much should be kept secret?

For the scrolls, which were formerly hidden away in the shadows, it is now necessary to strike a careful balance between the academic pursuit of knowledge and the ethical considerations of cultural preservation. In light of the fact that every choice they make will have repercussions throughout the fabric of history, the protagonist struggles to come to terms with the ramifications of their discovery.

Immediately following the revelation, the main character emerges from the concealed chambers, with scrolls in his hands and a fire of knowledge in his heart. What is found is a legacy that extends beyond the bounds of the archaeological expedition; it becomes a gift to humanity and a bridge between the modern and the old. The scrolls, which were formerly relegated to the shadows, now stand as blazing beacons that illuminate the ways through which human history has been constructed.

Both the burden of responsibility and the excitement of discovery are carried by the protagonist, who has been irrevocably altered as a result of the disclosures that occurred in the hidden chambers. It is a monument to the transformational force of archeological inquiry that the voyage, which is defined by twists of fate, linguistic hurdles, and ethical thoughts, becomes a journey.

The concealed chambers are no longer considered a secret enclave as the protagonist begins to reveal their discoveries to the rest of the world. The scrolls, which were once quiet witnesses to the passage of time, now reverberate with the voices of the past, echoing through the hallways of the current day. The voyage of the protagonist becomes a chapter in the ongoing story of human discovery, which is an exploration that continues to unravel the mysteries that are concealed within the folds of time. This odyssey takes place in the dance of shadows and light.

4.2 Narratives on governance, societal norms, and spiritual practices

A rich tapestry is created when government, societal norms, and spiritual practices converge. This tapestry is what stitches the fabric of human society together. These three pillars are intricately connected to one another, and hence influence and shape one another in a variety of different ways. The purpose of this investigation is to gain an understanding of the dynamic interactions that exist between these fundamental parts of human existence by delving into the tales that surround them.

The Narratives of Governance

Governance, at its most fundamental level, comprises the various systems and structures that civilizations apply in order to organize themselves. There are as many different perspectives on governance as there are kinds of civilizations that are governed. Over the course of history, from ancient civilizations to contemporary nation-states, the history of governance has been one of change, adaptation, and even revolution on occasion.

Narratives frequently center on the conflict that exists between freedom and authority when they are set within the setting of governance. A prime example of this conflict is the historical transition from monarchy to democracies across the globe. In the context of a larger narrative that strives to strike a balance between power between those who rule and those who are ruled, the Magna Carta, which was written in medieval England, the French Revolution, and the American Revolution are all examples.

As an additional point of interest, narratives on governance wrestle with issues pertaining to justice, equality, and the responsibility of the state in guaranteeing the well-being of its population. Concepts such as the social compact, which were initially defined by philosophers such as Hobbes, Locke, and Rousseau, offer a theoretical foundation for comprehending the legitimacy of political authority.

In more recent times, narratives on governance have broadened to include talks on global governance, human rights, and environmental stewardship. This expansion has occurred in response to globalization.

New narratives that transcend national borders and stress the interconnection of the global society are required in order to address the difficulties that the 21st century presents, which include climate change, pandemics, and economic inequality.

Perspectives on the Norms of Society

Human behavior within a certain community is governed by societal norms, which are the unwritten standards that regulate human behavior. These standards, which are frequently firmly rooted in cultural traditions, have the ability to alter the manner in which individuals interact with one another and with their surroundings. It is the values, expectations, and standards that societies hold dear that are reflected in the narratives that are told about society norms.

Among the several narratives that are prevalent in the sphere of societal norms is the conflict that exists between development and tradition. The difficulty of preserving cultural legacy while simultaneously adapting to changing conditions is one that societies struggle with continuously. This narrative is readily apparent in discussions concerning topics such as gender roles, family structures, and cultural traditions.

The narratives of social justice and human rights are also tightly connected to the development of societal standards since their inception. The standards that are currently in place that continue to perpetuate prejudice and injustice are being challenged by movements that advocate for civil rights, gender equality, and LGBTQ+ rights. The narratives presented here emphasize the significance of variety and inclusiveness in the process of developing societies that are more equal.

In addition, narratives concerning societal norms collide with these systems of the economy. For instance, the rise of capitalism has had an effect on the norms that society has established around individuality, competition, and consumption of many kinds. There is a need for a reassessment of the values that drive economic systems since critics say that these standards might contribute to social inequity and environmental destruction.

Narratives of practices that are spiritual

Whether they are organized religions or individual spiritual journeys, spiritual activities are intensely personal and frequently collective endeavors that strive to connect individuals with the transcendent. These practices can be found in both religious and spiritual contexts. There is a vast variety of ideas, rituals, and experiences that are included into narratives about spiritual practices. These practices have the ability to change the inner lives of individuals and communities.

The quest for meaning and purpose is a prominent story that may be found within the field of spiritual activities. When civilizations are going through rapid changes, individuals frequently turn to spiritual practices in order to gain a sense of transcendence and grounding in their lives. The resurgence of interest in mindfulness, meditation, and other contemplative practices in contemporary culture is a visible manifestation of this story.

In addition, the tales that accompany spiritual practices look into the connection that exists between religion and power relationships. Throughout the course of human history, religious organizations have been instrumental in the formation of laws, morals, and cultural standards thanks to their key position in governance. There is a narrative that strives to strike a balance between the principles of secular governance and the freedom of religion in many contemporary societies. This narrative is represented by the separation of church and state.

In addition, narratives on spiritual activities investigate the universal human need for transcendence and experiences that cannot be adequately described. Through various practices like prayer, meditation, and rituals, individuals strive to establish a connection with something that is more significant than themselves, so adding to a story that is not limited by cultural or religious borders.

There are tensions and intersections

The stories that are told about government, cultural norms, and spiritual practices do not exist in a vacuum; rather, they connect with one another and occasionally come into conflict with one another, resulting in tensions that will determine the path that human history takes. A good example of such an intersection is the connection that exists between government and the freedom of religion. In the narratives that are associated with this subject, the fights for religious tolerance and the safeguarding of individual beliefs against intrusion from the state are frequently highlighted.

In the field of social justice, the interaction between cultural norms and governance is another key junction that can be found. In this context, narratives investigate the ways in which laws and regulations can either reinforce or challenge the norms that are already in place in society, particularly those that continue to perpetuate discrimination on the basis of race, gender, or other social characteristics.

Moreover, in the framework of morals and ethics, spiritual practices tend to overlap with the standards that are prevalent in society. Frequently, narratives investigate the ways in which religious or spiritual beliefs have an impact on the actions of individuals as well as the values that society upholds. Debates on topics such as abortion, euthanasia, and bioethics can include a complicated interaction between religious views and secular standards of behavior.

Having a comprehensive awareness of the intricacies of human civilizations requires having a firm grasp on the narratives that pertain to government, cultural standards, and spiritual activities. They encapsulate the victories, hardships, and aspirations of various groups, reflecting the ever-changing character of human civilization and depicting the progression of human civilization. Although we are still in the process of navigating the issues of the present and the future, these narratives offer us a prism through which we can evaluate, critique, and imagine the societies that we want to create. Through the examination of these narratives, we are able to acquire a deeper understanding of the complex connection that exists between the political, social, and spiritual aspects of our collective human experience.

4.3 Unraveling the mystery behind the sudden disappearance of civilization

There have been several civilizations that have flourished and collapsed throughout the annals of human history. These civilizations have left behind relics, artifacts, and mysterious stories that serve as echoes of their existence. Particular cases in which entire civilizations appear to have vanished without a trace are among the chapters in this narrative that are both the most enthralling and the most confusing. For millennia, historians, archaeologists, and other academics have been captivated by the mysterious disappearance of societies such as the Indus Valley Civilization, the Maya, and the Anasazi. In the course of this investigation, we dive into the mystery that lies behind the unexpected loss of civilizations, making an effort to decipher the mystique that surrounds these lost societies.

"The Civilization of the Indus Valley"

The strange demise of the Indus Valley Civilization, which flourished between the years 3300 and 1300 BCE in the region that is now Pakistan and northwest India, is one of the oldest examples of a disappearance that is shrouded in mystery. An extensive urban planning system, sophisticated drainage systems, and a writing system that has not been deciphered to this day were all hallmarks of the Indus Valley Civilization when it was at its height. In spite of this, this once-thriving civilization started to fall apart around the year 1900 BCE.

The absence of clear proof or a single catastrophic event that led to the collapse is the source of the mystery that surrounds the collapse. There is an abundance of hypotheses, which range from natural changes, such as alterations in climate or tectonic activity, to socio-political reasons, such as invasions, internal disputes, or economic downfall. Due to the absence of a conclusive smoking gun, academics have been left with a lack of consensus regarding the final reason for the end of the Indus Valley Civilization. This has led to speculation and discussion among scholars.

The civilization of the Maya:

The Maya civilization, which flourished in the deep jungles of Mesoamerica between the years 250 and 900 CE, reached its point of greatest success. It appeared as though the Maya were unbeatable due to their great grasp of mathematics and astronomy, complicated city-states, and sophisticated hieroglyphic writing system. On the other hand, by the time the first millennium came to a close, their great cities had been deserted, and the civilization that had once flourished began to crumble.

There are many facets to the enigma that surrounds the fall of the Maya civilization when it was in existence. Deforestation and soil degradation are two examples of environmental issues that are thought to have contributed to the decline in agricultural production. In addition, there is evidence that city-states have been engaged in internal conflict and battle with one another. In spite of this, it does not appear that a single explanation is adequate to explain the sudden and widespread desertion of Maya municipalities. Various hypotheses propose that environmental stress, societal upheaval, and possibly the influence of external forces are all factors that contribute to the phenomenon.

The Anasazi people live in the American Southwest

Approximately between the years 200 and 1300 CE, the Anasazi people formed a complex society that flourished in the arid terrain of the American Southwest. They constructed exquisite cliff houses and developed intricate societies. However, the Anasazi people abandoned their cliff dwellings around the 13th century, leaving behind a mystery that has enthralled archaeologists and historians ever since.

A wide variety of hypotheses have been proposed to explain the disappearance of the Anasazi people. These hypotheses range from environmental factors, such as extended droughts, to sociopolitical factors, such as internal warfare or conflict. The depletion of resources or the effect of external forces, such as the introduction of new tribes, are two theories that have been proposed as possible contributors to their falling population. On the other hand, just like with other civilizations that have perished, a conclusive answer is still elusive.

Overarching Concepts and Obstacles in the Process of Deciphering Mysteries

There are a number of common themes and obstacles that emerge while attempting to unravel these mysteries, despite the fact that the specific circumstances surrounding the demise of each civilization are individually distinct.

Lack of Written Records: Many civilizations that have since perished have not left behind any written records or documents that explicitly outline the circumstances that led to their downfall. Attempts to reconstruct the tale are made more difficult by the absence of direct accounts; instead, they rely on archeological data, oral traditions, and interpretations of items.

In the ideas that have been proposed to explain the rapid extinction of civilizations, environmental factors play a significant role. Environmental changes and obstacles are featured extensively. Changes in climate, droughts, deforestation, and the deterioration of soil are among factors that have been suggested as possible contributors. It's possible that these variables caused a tremendous amount of stress on agricultural systems and the availability of resources, which ultimately led to the collapse of society.

Internal disputes, warfare, and social upheaval are recurrent elements in the tales of vanished civilizations. Socio Political dynamics are associated with these recurring themes. It's possible that internal conflicts for resources, power, and influence could have contributed to the destabilization of societies, which would have ultimately led to their demise.

External Factors: When discussing the collapse of civilization, it is common practice to take into account the impact of external factors, such as invasions or migrations of other people. It is possible that the entrance of new populations or the incursion of external forces were factors that contributed to the downfall of indigenous civilizations. These factors may have caused existing social structures to become disorganized.

As a result of the complexity of the factors involved, the collapse of a civilization is rarely explained by a single factor. As an alternative, it is possible that environmental, social, and economic forces will come together to form a complex web of obstacles that will contribute to the disintegration of society.

When it comes to the study of human history, one of the most intriguing mysteries that continues to be a mystery is the unexpected extinction of civilizations. The history of the Indus Valley Civilization, the Maya, and the Anasazi, amongst others, give a tantalizing challenge to researchers who are attempting to comprehend the mechanisms of the collapse of societies. Despite the abundance of hypotheses, the absence of conclusive evidence and the complex nature of these collapses continue to make it difficult to provide straightforward answers.

A multidisciplinary approach that incorporates archaeological results, environmental science, anthropology, and historical research is required in order to unravel the riddle that lies behind the rapid extinction of civilizations. It is possible that our understanding of these extinct societies will develop as a result of technological advancements and new discoveries.

This will provide us with valuable new insights into the intricate interplay of causes that contributed to the mysterious fall of these societies. Not only does the pursuit of these riddles deepen our understanding of the past, but it also compels us to think on the resiliency and fragility of human civilizations throughout the course of history.

4.4 Clashes with a secret society determined to keep the truth hidden

Through the centuries, the human imagination has been intrigued by stories of secret organizations that weave intricate webs to conceal hidden facts. These stories take place in the murky area that exists between reality and conspiracy. A recurrent motif in works of literature, folklore, and speculative fiction is the conflict that arises between individuals who are interested in discovering the truth and private groups that are adamant about concealing it. The purpose of this investigation is to delve into the fictional narrative of people or groups uncovering secrets that a mysterious society seeks to keep hidden from the public eye.

A Shroud of Confidentiality

At the core of the story is the cloak of secrecy that envelops the covert organization and the covert goals it seeks to accomplish. This shadowy organization, which is sometimes represented as an old and powerful institution, is responsible for manipulating the course of events by pulling threads when they are not visible to the naked eye. The organization's members are skilled at concealing their genuine identities and purposes, and the organization's motives are poorly understood.

The story often begins with the introduction of protagonists, who may be journalists, investigators, or anyone with a strong sense of curiosity. These protagonists are the ones who discover clues or anomalies that hint at a more profound and concealed reality. As they follow these breadcrumbs, they find themselves in a rabbit hole of mystery, where they discover truths that call into question previously held beliefs and pose a danger to the very foundation of the society in which they are embedded.

Controversies with those who seek the truth

The heroes, as they continue to peel back layers of deception, find themselves becoming adversaries of the secret organization without even realizing it. The conflict becomes more intense when the individuals who are seeking the truth unearth facts that would be detrimental to the organization's vested interests. The society, on the other hand, makes use of a variety of strategies in order to frustrate their investigations, producing a story that is fraught with suspense and includes elements of danger, moral ambiguity, and intrigue.

The secret society is quite skilled in the art of deceit, and they are also very good at misdirection.

False leads, red herrings, and information that is both misleading and misleading are carefully provided in order to deflect those who are looking for the truth from their quest. The characters are forced to navigate a complex maze of illusions and half-truths, and they are never sure who they can put their faith in.

Intimidation and Coercion: The covert organization uses intimidation and coercion as a means of guaranteeing the confidentiality of its information. In order to prevent the protagonists from venturing further into prohibited zones, it is necessary to use methods that threaten their lives, the lives of their loved ones, or their reputations. In this story, the distinction between ally and foe becomes more hazy, which adds an additional layer of psychological complexity.

The digital era has transformed technology into a battlefield, and this is known as technological warfare. In order to exert control over the narrative, the secret society, which is equipped with highly developed technology skills, does things like hacking, surveillance, and information manipulation. The people who are looking for the truth need to make use of their own technological capabilities in order to outwit their opponents.

Historical Manipulation: The secret society frequently conceals long-forgotten secrets or historical realities that, if ever revealed, have the potential to change the narratives that have been formed. When it comes to the conflict, the manipulation of historical records, artifacts, or information becomes an essential component. By utilizing their knowledge of history, the characters are tasked with distinguishing between the authentic and the fake.

The heroes either infiltrate the secret society or vice versa, which is a classic aspect of the narrative. Espionage is another element that contributes to the narrative. Espionage, disguises, and undercover operations are all elements that are utilized by both sides in order to acquire insights into the plans of the other. In this situation, loyalty is put to the test, and betrayal becomes an ever-present danger.

Themes that are Analyzed in the Conflict

Throughout the course of the conflict, the story delves into a number of topics that strike a chord with viewers and appeal to their common curiosity with concealed information, power conflicts, and the repercussions of uncovering the truth.

The topic of power and control lies at the heart of the conflict that has arisen between the two parties. The secret society, which is frequently portrayed as having enormous influence, is attempting to preserve the status quo by keeping its confidential information a secret.

These power dynamics are challenged by the protagonists, who are motivated by a desire for justice or enlightenment, and in the process, they put everything on the balance.

Ethical Conundrums: The conflict presents the protagonists with ethical conundrums that drive them to confront the repercussions of their goal. In light of the possible damage that it could do, is the truth worth it? Should there be any information that is kept secret for the sake of the greater good? The narrative struggles with moral ambiguity, which proves to be tough not just for the characters but also for the audience.

The conflict frequently involves the idea of reality vs perception, which is a notion that is frequently played with. Established narratives are called into question, and the protagonists contest the facts that are generally accepted in their environment. The narrative prompts the viewer to contemplate the extent to which their own reality may be influenced by influences that are concealed from view or perceptions that have been altered.

There is a price to pay for knowledge, and that price is the pursuit of the truth. The conflict investigates the personal, professional, and existential sacrifices that the protagonists have made throughout the story. As the protagonists make their way through the perilous path of enlightenment, the weight of knowledge and the responsibility that it entails become prominent themes.

Symbolism and Allegory: In order to successfully communicate more profound meanings, the narrative frequently makes use of symbolism and allegory. One interpretation of the secret society is that it represents the covert forces that exert control over society, while the protagonists represent the innate human desire for knowledge and freedom. As a metaphor for the never-ending conflict between enlightenment and ignorance, the clash becomes a metaphor.

An example of a narrative archetype that is universally applicable across all cultures and time periods is the conflict with a secret society that is adamant about concealing the truth. It appeals to the most fundamental aspects of human nature, such as the need to acquire information, the search for justice, and the confrontation with the unknown. This narrative crafts a tapestry of mystery, peril, and the enduring human spirit, regardless of whether it takes place in the distant past, the present day, or a hypothetical future.

As the audience interacts with these stories, they are prompted to rethink their own conceptions of reality, to contemplate the repercussions of uncovering concealed facts, and to contemplate the delicate balance that exists between enlightenment and the maintenance of society order. Storytelling becomes a vehicle for examining the complexities of the human condition when it comes into conflict with a secret society. It invites us to cast our gaze into the shadows and discover the mysteries that lay beneath the surface of our collective consciousness.

Chapter 5

Guardians of the Past

The past acts as a repository for memories, lessons, and cultural treasures, which are all interwoven into the intricate tapestry that is the human experience. The people who are responsible for this legacy, who are frequently referred to as "Guardians of the Past," play an essential part in ensuring that the richness of history is preserved and protected for both the current generation and the generations to come. The purpose of this investigation is to investigate the myriad of obligations, difficulties, and significance that are associated with people who have been entrusted with the responsibility of protecting our common legacy.

The Functions of Those Who Watch Over the Past

Archivists and curators are the individuals who are responsible for upholding the preservation of historical records and artifacts. Collections of objects, papers, and artworks are methodically cataloged, preserved, and shown by these devoted specialists who work at cultural institutions such as museums, libraries, archives, and other academic institutions. In addition to their job as curators, they also play the duty of guardians of cultural narratives, ensuring that the tangible and intangible history of civilizations is safeguarded from the destructive effects of time.

Academics and Historians: Historians and academics fulfill the role of intellectual guardians by delving into the annals of the past in order to unearth concealed tales, unravel puzzles, and give historical events with context. By conducting research, conducting analysis, and documenting historical accounts, they make a contribution to the overall comprehension of human history. The foundation upon which narratives about the past are formed, tested, and developed is the job that they have done.

Individuals and organizations of people all around the world take on the role of cultural preservationists in order to protect the customs, languages, and practices that have been passed down through generations in a variety of different cultures. These guardians frequently operate within their communities, with the goal of ensuring that the knowledge and customs of their ancestors are passed down to all subsequent generations. The efforts that they make guarantee that the cultural fabric of societies will continue to be alive and tied to its founding principles.

The physical vestiges of the past, such as architectural marvels and heritage sites, require vigilant care in order to endure the impacts of time and environmental variables.

Architects and conservators are responsible for this. A guardian role is played by architects and conservators, who are responsible for monitoring the restoration and conservation of historical structures. Through their efforts, they ensure that future generations will have the opportunity to observe and appreciate the architectural accomplishments of historical eras.

Librarians and Information Specialists: In this day and age, when information is becoming more and more digital, librarians and information specialists play the role of protectors of knowledge. They are responsible for managing huge archives of books, manuscripts, and digital resources, which allows them to make knowledge available while also ensuring that the assets are preserved in their original state. In order to cultivate a culture that values learning and intellectual curiosity, their involvement is of the utmost importance.

What Obstacles Do Guardians of the Past Have to Overcome?

Threats to the Environment: The physical objects and structures that date back to the past are susceptible to environmental dangers such as pollution, natural catastrophes, and climate change. The destruction of cultural heritage can be accelerated by factors such as rising sea levels, extreme weather events, and air pollution, which presents issues for those who are responsible with the preservation of cultural heritage.

Because of technological obsolescence, the difficulty of keeping digital data and resources and gaining access to them is becoming increasingly difficult as technology continues to advance forward. There are a number of challenges that digital archives must face, including the degradation of data, the evolution of file formats, and the rapid obsolescence of hardware and software. All of these challenges have the potential to affect the accessibility of digital archives over the long run.

Financing and Resources: Many organizations that are responsible for the preservation of the past are housed within institutions that are dependent on receiving financing for their work. The implementation of comprehensive conservation and restoration projects might be hampered by limited financial resources, which in turn hinders the ability to safeguard and promote historical assets.

Cultural and Political Obstacles: The preservation of the past can be made more difficult in certain circumstances due to the presence of cultural or political variables. There is a possibility that historical monuments, relics, or traditions could be endangered by conflicts, wars, or ideological disputes. In order to successfully navigate these issues, it is necessary to strike a delicate balance between the imperative of preservation and the intricacies of the circumstance that exists now.

In situations when the repatriation of cultural items or human remains is at stake, guardians of the past frequently find themselves in situations that present them with ethical dilemmas. Questions pertaining to ownership, cultural sensitivity, and the rights of indigenous populations to reclaim their legacy call for careful analysis and collaborative effort.

The Significance of Being a Guardianage

Cultural Continuity: The guardians of the past play a crucial role in ensuring that cultural continuity is maintained. One way in which they contribute to the sense of identification and belonging that exists within communities is through the preservation of languages, traditions, and practices. It is via this continuity that a connection is fostered between generations of the past, present, and future.

The educational value of historical objects, papers, and sites is that they are extremely valuable instructional resources. In addition to providing a concrete connection to the events, innovations, and accomplishments that have formed societies, guardians of the past also create possibilities for learning and inspiration. Archives, museums, and other cultural institutions transform into living schools that are not bound by the passage of time.

Communal Memory: The protection of the past is something that is absolutely necessary in order to keep communal memory intact. The guardians of historical knowledge assist societies to remember their victories, their challenges, and the lessons they have learned from the past by conserving and sharing relevant historical information. Through the use of this collective memory, a basis for the growth and resilience of society is established.

Cultural interaction and Tourism: Historical places and artifacts that have been well kept are able to attract tourists and create opportunities for cultural interaction. There is a correlation between the preservation of history and the global appreciation of other cultures, which in turn helps to cultivate mutual respect and understanding. A bridge that is able to traverse both geographical and temporal borders is something that cultural heritage can become.

Inspiring Creativity and Innovation: The past is a rich source of inspiration for creative and innovative endeavors. Through the provision of insights into historical accomplishments, scientific developments, and artistic expressions, guardians of the past make a contribution to the creative process. Understanding what happened in the past provides fuel for the imagination and encourages invention in a variety of sectors.

The duty of Guardians of the Past is one that is not only a difficult task but also a responsibility of the highest kind.

These individuals negotiate a landscape that is loaded with problems in order to protect our collective legacy. These challenges range from environmental dangers to ethical considerations. But the stories, objects, and traditions that define who we are as individuals and as a global society are irreplaceable, and their efforts are very necessary to ensure that they are preserved.

When we recognize the significance of guardianship, it becomes clear that the past is not a static entity but rather a dynamic force that changes our present and informs our future. This reveals that the past is not a static object. The people who are responsible for preserving history, culture, and heritage act as guiding lights, directing us through the passageways of time and making certain that the reverberations of the past continue to resonate for future generations. Our collective human history is able to maintain its continuity, relevance, and enduring significance while it is in the hands of these guardians.

5.1 Introduction of a group protecting the secrets of the Indus Valley Civilization

The enigmatic Indus Valley Civilization is a mystery that has fascinated historians, archaeologists, and explorers for centuries. It is located in the center of the Indian subcontinent, where the ancient river systems once hosted a civilization that was unsurpassed in its level of sophistication. This advanced society flourished from approximately 3300 BCE to 1300 BCE, and it left behind the relics of cities that were painstakingly built, a written script that has not yet been fully deciphered, and a plethora of artifacts that hint at a sophistication that belies its age.

In the midst of the intrigue that surrounds the Indus Valley Civilization, a dark collective that is dedicated to safeguarding the mysteries and secrets that the ancient civilization possesses has emerged as a covert society. The purpose of this investigation is to look into the fictional narrative of the introduction of a group that is known as the "Keepers of the Silent Cities." This group is a secret organization that is dedicated to protecting the mysteries of the Indus Valley Civilization from the prying eyes of the modern world.

When the Keepers were first born

In the legacy of old wisdom and the protection of historical truths, the Keepers of the Silent Cities have their roots deeply rooted in the past. A group of individuals, each of whom possessed a distinct blend of skills in archaeology, linguistics, and ancient history, came together throughout the 20th century, which brought to a renewed interest in the Indus Valley Civilization as well as scholarly investigation into it. They were brought together by a common respect for the mysteries of the past, and it was with this respect that they founded the Keepers in order to guarantee the protection of the civilization's secrets.

The founding members of the Keepers bring a wide range of skills to the table, which is a positive aspect of the organization. Archaeologists who are well-versed in the excavation of ancient ruins, linguists who are seeking to interpret the mysterious Indus script, and historians who have a profound understanding of the society structures that existed during that time period are the primary members of this covert organization. Every member of the group possesses a key that can be used to unlock a particular facet of the ancient mysteries.

The Keepers are united by a common goal, which is to preserve the authenticity of the legacy left behind by the Indus Valley Civilization. The Keepers are motivated by the conviction that the secrets of this ancient culture have the ability to transform our understanding of history. As a result, they regard themselves as guardians of a cultural and intellectual treasure trove that must be protected at all costs.

Historical obligation The Keepers, who consider themselves to be the guardians of history, are burdened with the weight of a significant obligation. They are of the opinion that the secrets that are buried within the silent cities could have far-reaching ramifications for the present and the future, changing the trajectory of academic debate, cultural narratives, and even the dynamics of geopolitical situations.

Modus operandi and the Mission Statement

As they navigate the delicate balance between the need to conserve ancient mysteries and the pursuit of knowledge, the Keepers of the Silent Cities function with a covert precision. Their goal is shrouded in secrecy, and they operate with a precision that remains hidden from the public.

Stealth and incognito: The Keepers are able to operate in the shadows while continuing to retain their tight incognito. The identity of these individuals are meticulously concealed, and the actions that they engage in are shrouded in a web of secrecy. Not only is this anonymity a practical measure, but it is also an intentional tactic made with the intention of protecting the Keepers from potential threats and pressures from the outside world.

Surveillance and Counterintelligence: The Keepers make use of sophisticated surveillance and counterintelligence capabilities in order to safeguard the secrets that they are responsible for guarding. They are skilled at identifying and foiling efforts to infiltrate their ranks or get access to their concealed knowledge vaults. They are aware that their purpose leaves them susceptible to meddling from other sources.

With regard to selective disclosure, the Keepers are aware of the delicate balance that must be maintained between the preservation of the past and the potential advantages of disclosed information. While they are steadfast in their determination to safeguard the most important secrets of the Indus Valley Civilization, they deliberate about the potential repercussions of divulging particular findings that have the potential to improve humanity's comprehension without putting the most closely held mysteries of civilization in jeopardy.

Artifact Recovery: In a world where ancient artifacts are highly sought after by collectors, museums, and scholars alike, the Keepers are actively engaged in the process of recovering items from the Indus Valley Civilization that have been misplaced or stolen. Through the use of their global network, they are able to prevent the illegal transfer of these historical artifacts, ensuring that they continue to be under the watchful eye of the Keepers.

Understanding the significance of diplomatic maneuvering, the Keepers build relationships and influence among academic circles, cultural organizations, and even government agencies. They do this because they are aware of the value of maneuvering diplomatically. The objective of these individuals is to mold the narratives that surround the ancient civilization and to protect themselves from potential dangers posed by entities that have competing interests.

The Obstacles That the Keepers Must Overcome

As they navigate the complex terrain of academia, geopolitics, and the unrelenting march of time, the Keepers of the Silent Cities are confronted with a multitude of problems due to the hidden nature of their organization.

There is no way to avoid the presence of external dangers when one is responsible for the protection of old secrets. The mysteries of the Indus Valley Civilization are being unraveled by ambitious archaeologists, unscrupulous collectors, or competing groups for the sake of gaining personal riches, academic prestige, or even geopolitical advantage.

Internal Rifts: Although the Keepers' diverse knowledge originally served as a source of strength, it has the potential to also cause internal rifts within the organization. There is a possibility that the cohesiveness of the organization could be strained due to differences in interpretation, priorities, or ethical issues, which would then raise doubts regarding the most effective way to carry out their purpose.

Challenges Presented by Technology The Keepers are confronted with a multifaceted dilemma as a result of the rapid growth of technology. On the one hand, it provides new instruments for the management of historical information and the dissemination of such information.

On the other hand, it raises the possibility of leaks, whether accidental or intentional, that might put the confidentiality of the ancient secrets at risk.

Disclosure Striking the Right Balance The Keepers face a continuing problem in maintaining a balance between the preservation of the past and the dissemination of their knowledge to the larger world. As the global scene continues to change, the ethical issues that are involved in selective disclosure need to be reevaluated on a consistent basis.

Conundrums with Ethical Implications The Keepers' mission, by its very nature, presents them with ethical conundrums. In order to make decisions regarding which secrets to safeguard, which artifacts to recover, and how much information to disclose, they need to do a complicated moral calculation that takes into account the potential impact on humanity's understanding of its history.

What the Keepers' Mission Means and Why It Is Important

Preservation of Cultural Identity The secrets that are kept by the Keepers are not only historical curiosities; rather, they represent an essential component of the cultural identity of the areas that were formerly occupied by the Indus Valley Civilization. As a result of their efforts to protect these secrets, the Keepers make a significant contribution to the maintenance of cultural continuity and the resilience of communities that are related to this historic legacy.

In an era in which archaeological sites and artifacts are vulnerable to exploitation, the Keepers serve as a bulwark against the plundering of the past. They provide protection against the exploitation of the past. They defend the silent towns from becoming nothing more than commodities by preventing the transmission of illegal goods and ensuring that historical places are preserved in their original state.

The Keepers are guarding secrets that have the capacity to modify societal narratives and challenge established paradigms. This potential for societal transformation gives the Keepers the ability to transform society. These discoveries, if selectively disclosed, have the potential to stimulate societal revolution, thereby encouraging fresh perspectives on government, urban development, and cultural interchange.

Ensuring the Protection of Intellectual Property The intellectual treasures that are contained within the silent cities are susceptible to being misinterpreted or inappropriately appropriated. In order to ensure that the information that has been obtained from the past is handled with care and that the intricacies and complexity of the Indus Valley Civilization are respected, the Keepers perform a crucial role.

Inspiration for Future Generations The Keepers, in their role as guardians of the past, serve as a source of inspiration for future generations, encouraging them to recognize the significance of maintaining cultural heritage and the value of historical knowledge. By preserving the mysteries of the Indus Valley Civilization, they arouse curiosity and reverence for the tales that are concealed within the cities that are quiet.

The introduction of the Keepers of the Silent Cities creates a rich tapestry of mystery, responsibility, and the delicate dance that takes place between the protection of secrets and the possibility of revelations that can bring about transformation. To maintain the heritage of an ancient civilization that has been whispering its secrets for millennia, the Keepers stand as guardians in the murky passages where history and the present collide. They bear the weight of a tremendous responsibility to protect the legacy of this old civilization. The Keepers are navigating a maze of hurdles, ethical issues, and the never-ending desire to strike a balance between the preservation of the past, the necessities of the present, and the ambitions of the future as their story develops.

5.2 Protagonist faces challenges and threats from the clandestine organization

When it comes to suspenseful narratives and thrilling stories, the conflict that arises between a motivated protagonist and a secret organization adds layers of interest and depth to the story that is unfolding. In the course of the protagonist's efforts to unearth secrets that have been concealed in the shadows, they are required to cross a perilous landscape that is filled with difficulties and threats offered by the covert organization. This investigation goes into the captivating storyline of a main character who is confronted by a secret organization, revealing a complex web of deception, danger, and mystery.

Uncovering the Mystery Through the Actor of the Story

The protagonist is a character whose journey becomes the focal point of the story. This figure is at the center of the narrative. There are certain characteristics that the protagonist possesses that put them on a collision course with the covert organization. These characteristics include the fact that the protagonist is either an investigative journalist, a historian, or an ordinary person who is thrown into exceptional circumstances. A personal connection to the secrets held by the organization, an insatiable curiosity, or a desire for justice are all examples of attributes that may be present in the individual.

Backstory and Motivation: The backstory of the protagonist frequently becomes intertwined with the overarching mystery, which propels them into the center of the struggle. The protagonist is driven to confront the secret organization by a combination of personal reasons, unsolved traumas, or a profound yearning for truth. These are the driving forces that lead the protagonist this way.

Capabilities and Expertise: The protagonist possesses a collection of abilities or expertise that proves to be essential in the process of uncovering the secrets of the organization. The toolset of the protagonist becomes crucial in order for them to successfully navigate the problems that they face, regardless of whether it is investigation skill, linguistic ability, technological savvy, or physical strength respectively.

Moral Compass: The protagonist's moral compass acts as a guiding force, separates them from the secret organization, and serves as a distinguishing factor. They find that their dedication to justice, truth, or a higher ethical code serves as a source of strength for them when they confront the ethical conundrums that are presented to them by their voyage.

The protagonist possesses a number of distinguishing characteristics, one of which is resilience, which can be defined as the resistance to give in to threats or intimidation. A layer of tension and suspense is added to the story by the protagonist's commitment to see the quest through to its conclusion, despite the growing number of challenges.

It is the clandestine organization known as the architects of shadows

The mysterious group that is the adversary of the protagonist is the clandestine organization, which is a shadowy collective that has a vested interest in maintaining control and security. The operations of this group are extremely precise, and they employ a wide variety of strategies in order to conceal their goal. It is possible that the organization is of a variety of natures, ranging from a covert society that protects old information to a contemporary conspiracy that manipulates international politics.

Motives That Are Shrouded in Mysteries The motivations of the covert organization are frequently disguised so that they are surrounded by multiple levels of intrigue. It is unclear if their acts are motivated by a desire for power, the preservation of old secrets, or the pursuit of a hidden purpose; yet, the fact that they continue to conceal their deeds serves to strengthen the protagonist's resolve to discover the truth.

The group thrives on maintaining operational secrecy, which is essential to its success. The members of this organization go about their business in the shadows, keeping their identities a secret and directing events with such exquisite precision that they keep the protagonist guessing. As the story progresses, the protagonist is forced to negotiate a world in which each new discovery raises new questions.

Mastery of Technology: In this day and age, technology has evolved into a powerful instrument that provides the covert organization with a competitive advantage.

They have access to hacking, surveillance, and the manipulation of information because they have these capabilities. There are obstacles that the protagonist must overcome in order to successfully navigate a digital terrain in which the organization's technological expertise offers a persistent danger.

Both infiltration and espionage are areas in which the organization succeeds exceptionally well. Secret monitoring, misleading strategies, and agents working within the protagonist's closest circle all contribute to the creation of an atmosphere of mistrust. The protagonist is forced to contend with the challenge of determining who exactly is a friend and who is an enemy.

Coercion and Intimidation: In order to safeguard its confidential information, the organization resorts to using coercion and being intimidating. Threats against the life of the protagonist, the safety of loved ones, or the revelation of personal vulnerabilities are effective techniques that are used to prevent the protagonist from conducting an investigation into the matter.

The Obstacles That the Protagonist Experiences

As the protagonist sets out on their adventure to discover the secrets that are being guarded by the secret organization, they come across a number of obstacles that put their tenacity and determination to the test.

Asymmetry of Information: The clandestine organization is able to function with a significant advantage, which is information asymmetry. Within the context of the story, the protagonist is confronted with the problem of putting together pieces of information while simultaneously battling an adversary who is in possession of the key to essential insights.

Constant Surveillance: The main character is constantly being watched by the secret organization that is involved in the secret organization. The presence of surveillance, whether it be digital or real, adds an additional element of vulnerability and paranoia. It is difficult to think and prepare without informing the organization of their plans because every action is analyzed, which makes it difficult to execute.

The protagonist must negotiate a terrain in which allies may turn out to be double agents. Betrayal and double agents are important aspects of this landscape. In order to add an element of unpredictability to the story, the protagonist is forced to reassess their loyalties and alliances when they are betrayed by someone within their inner circle.

The clandestine group uses psychological warfare in order to wear down the protagonist's determination along the course of the story. Destabilizing the mental and emotional fortitude of the protagonist can be accomplished through the use of strategies such as mind games, manipulation, and the resurfacing of past traumatic experiences.

Pursuit and Physical Threats: Both of these elements raise the stakes for the protagonist by increasing the likelihood of them being pursued. The confrontations with agents of the covert organization become increasingly intense, resulting in tense encounters, narrow escapes, and the ongoing sense that their lives are in imminent danger.

Topics that are Investigated During the Protagonist's Adventure

It is the search for truth that serves as the driving force behind the journey that the protagonist takes along the way. The narrative investigates the extent to which the protagonist is ready to go in order to expose hidden realities, thereby undermining conventional narratives and putting the protagonist's personal safety at danger in the pursuit of enlightenment.

Individual against Institution: The power dynamics that are at play are brought to light by the power struggle that takes place between the individual protagonist and the intimidating anonymous organization. Resistance against repressive institutions, the resiliency of the individual, and the quest for autonomy are all themes that are woven throughout the narrative.

In the course of navigating a landscape in which the boundary between right and wrong is hazy, the protagonist is confronted with a number of ethical conundrums. Decisions that could result in the disclosure of confidential information, the occurrence of collateral damage, and the question of whether or not their acts are moral become defining moments in the narrative.

Legacy and Impact: The secrets that are guarded by the secret organization frequently have far-reaching effects either for the protagonist, for society, or even for the globe as a whole. The protagonist is forced to confront the weight of their discoveries, which allows for the exploration of themes such as legacy, impact, and the responsibility that comes with owning possession of knowledge.

Metamorphosis and Resilience: The trials that are presented by the covert organization serve as a crucible for the metamorphosis that the protagonist undergoes. As a result of the protagonist's development in response to the growing dangers, the tale incorporates themes of resiliency, adaptability, and the capacity for growth under duress. These themes are important to the narrative.

There are elements of mystery, suspense, and psychological depth that are painted onto the canvas of the storytelling in the captivating story of a protagonist who is confronted with obstacles and threats from a covert organization. The narrative tension that is created as a result of the conflict between the unrelenting individual who is always looking for the truth and the shadowy organization that uses concealment as its weapon is what keeps spectators interested.

The journey of the protagonist resonates with themes of morality, individual agency, and the desire of enlightenment, which invites the spectator to contemplate the complexities of the human experience as it develops. Within the intricate dance that takes place between light and shadow, the adventure of the protagonist transforms into an enthralling investigation of bravery, self-sacrifice, and the unending search for a truth that has the potential to remain forever concealed within the depths of secrecy.

5.3 Delve into the moral dilemma of revealing the truth versus preserving secrets

There is a profound moral conundrum that arises from the ongoing conflict between the urge to expose the truth and the imperative to keep secrets hidden. This conflict is woven into the delicate fabric of human existence. This ethical conundrum, which is intertwined into the fabric of personal relationships, societal systems, and historical narratives, encourages meditation on the intricacies of disclosure and the repercussions of shielding some truths from public view. As we continue to go deeper into this moral maze, we will investigate the conflict that exists between openness and discretion, and we will struggle with the myriad of factors that influence decisions surrounding the disclosure or concealment of secrets.

What is the nature of the truth and secrets?

The pursuit of truth is sometimes hailed as a moral undertaking, a path to enlightenment and liberation. Truth is commonly referred to as the "truth." Truth is considered as a basis for trust and authenticity in personal interactions, which helps to establish true connections within the context of those relationships. When viewed in a broader context, the disclosure of truths has the potential to result in societal advancement, justice, and a populace that is better educated.

The role of Secrets as Guardians On the other hand, secrets are frequently seen to be guardians of privacy, autonomy, and the maintenance of individual or community well-being. Individuals are able to navigate their internal landscapes without the judgment of others when they reveal personal secrets, which protect them from vulnerabilities. When it comes to the spheres of politics and diplomacy, societal secrets are considered to be essential for the purpose of preserving an atmosphere of stability and security.

The Truth's Place in the Moral Imperative:

Integrity and Trust: The moral responsibility to expose the truth is rooted in the concepts of trust and integrity from the very beginning. When it comes to personal relationships, hiding important facts can be detrimental to trust, which can ultimately result in fractures in the foundation of the connection. When it comes to the public realm, institutions that are built on honesty and transparency are considered to be the cornerstones of ethical governance.

Accountability and Justice: The disclosure of the truth is considered to be a fundamental component of both accountability and justice. In the framework of the judicial system, the hiding of facts or the lack of disclosure of evidence can undermine the efforts to achieve justice. When it comes to maintaining fairness and holding individuals or organizations accountable for their actions, the disclosure of the truth becomes a moral obligation.

On an individual level, the truth is frequently regarded as a catalyst for personal growth and healing. This is because the truth is the truth. Self-discovery and emotional catharsis are two outcomes that can result from confronting realities that are uncomfortable, admitting to having made mistakes, and embracing emotional vulnerability. In this view, the pursuit of truth is congruent with a more general moral obligation to promote both individual and societal well-being.

The Moral Difficulty Involved in the Security of Secrets:

Protection of Privacy: The moral need to safeguard privacy is inextricably linked to the practice of keeping secrets concealed. persons have the right to protect certain elements of their lives from being scrutinized by the public, and the act of keeping secrets becomes an ethical act when it protects the autonomy and dignity of persons.

For the sake of maintaining national security and stability, it is acceptable for certain secrets to be kept secret at the society level. This is because certain secrets are necessary for maintaining national security. The protection of classified information in the fields of military, intelligence, and diplomacy is frequently practiced in order to avoid causing harm to civilians and to preserve the equilibrium of geopolitical affairs. The ethical requirement in this situation is to exercise appropriate stewardship of information for the benefit of society as a whole.

A moral need to reduce the amount of harm that is caused may be the driving force behind the decision to keep secrets. There is a possibility that the disclosure of particular truths could result in severe repercussions, either on an individual or social level. The ethical consideration is comparing the potential benefits that could be brought about by the disclosure of information against the potential harm that could be caused by the disclosure.

Finding Your Way Through the Moral Terrain:

Contextual ethics refers to the moral conundrum that arises when confronted with the decision of whether to reveal or keep secrets. The ethical implications of a specific circumstance are contingent upon a number of elements, including cultural standards, the classification of the information, and the potential outcomes that could result from its revelation. It is possible that anything that is considered morally justified in one setting could be considered unethical in another.

Outcomes and Intentions: The moral appraisal of activities that are related to truth and secrets frequently depends on the intentions that lie behind those actions as well as the outcomes that are predictable. It is possible to weigh the intentions to protect, preserve, or shield against the potential harm that could be created by delaying the disclosure of the truth. A nuanced evaluation of ethical standards is required in order to strike a balance between these considerations.

Temporal Considerations The passage of time can change the moral calculus of whether or not to divulge secrets or to keep them a secret. Something that was once considered to be sensitive or hurtful may, as time passes, lose its weight in terms of ethical considerations. On the other hand, the revelation of certain facts had the potential to acquire significance as the historical context developed.

Dilemmas of Moral Importance in Real Life and in Fiction:

Investigations in Literature The ethical conundrum that arises from the relationship between truth and secrets has been a recurrent motif in literary works. Characters are forced to make choices that have the potential to change the trajectory of their own life as well as the lives of others. The tension between revelation and preservation becomes a narrative crucible in a wide variety of forms of literature, ranging from Shakespearean tragedies to contemporary psychological thrillers.

Throughout the course of history, there have been several instances in which individuals, countries, and leaders have been confronted with ethical conundrums about the revelation or concealment of different types of information. The delicate interplay between moral imperatives and pragmatic factors is brought into sharper focus by decisions that are taken during times of war, political turmoil, or social revolution.

When it comes to the delicate dance of ethics, the moral conundrum of whether or not to expose the truth or to keep secrets requires careful consideration. The conflict that is inherent in this ethical conundrum is a reflection of the intricacy of human interactions, the structures of society, and the ever-changing fact that truth itself is constantly altering.

Despite the fact that individuals and society are struggling with decisions that require the disclosure or concealment of information, the moral landscape continues to be fluid and dynamic. A prudent balancing of conflicting values, an understanding of the contextual nuances at play, and a recognition of the ever-changing character of moral imperatives are all necessary components in the quest of an ethical equilibrium.

Ultimately, the moral dilemma surrounding truth and secrets invites individuals to engage in a profound introspection about the principles that guide their actions, the responsibilities that come with knowledge, and the enduring quest for a moral compass that can navigate the labyrinthine terrain of human morality. In the course of this continuing investigation, the moral tightrope that individuals and society must walk with discernment and ethical thought is the delicate balance that exists between the disclosure of truth and the protection of secrets.

5.4 A journey through remote locations, ancient caves, and forgotten temples

The act of embarking on a journey that takes one through distant areas, ancient caves, and forgotten temples is not only a physical undertaking; rather, it is a journey into the heart of history and mystery. Remains of long-vanished civilizations, echoes of stories that have not been recounted, and the reverberations of spiritual sanctuaries can be found in the secluded regions of the planet, where time appears to have stopped standing still. The purpose of this investigation is to uncover the intricate web of such a journey, which is a search for the forgotten that promises to bring about discovery, adventure, and a profound connection with previous times.

Portals to the unknown can be found in remote locations.

Separated Wilderness: The voyage starts in the embrace of a wilderness that is completely separated from the rest of the world, where nature is the master and human presence is a mere whisper. There are doors to the unknown that can be found in these remote regions, which are unaffected by the hustle and bustle of modern life. The story is brought to life on a canvas that comprises barren landscapes, craggy mountain ranges, and dense forests.

The concept of cultural isolation refers to the fact that certain remote regions are not only geographically isolated but also culturally distinct. In certain parts of the world, rituals, traditions, and ways of life that date back centuries have been passed down from generation to generation. The voyage through such locations transforms into a cultural expedition, providing glimpses into ways of living that have withstood the passage of time.

Hidden Communities: In the midst of the isolation, there are communities that are hidden from view, and only a select few are aware of their existence.

The tour transforms into a respectful investigation of these communities, with the goal of establishing connections and understanding while treading softly on the delicate fabric of their lives.

Caves from the past are gateways to mystifying underground worlds.

Subterranean treasures: Exploring old caverns is like taking a step down into the subterranean treasures that the Earth has to offer her inhabitants. These tunnels, which have been sculpted by the hands of time, contain mysteries that have been kept hidden for decades or even centuries. The geological history of the world can be uncovered via the examination of chambers that are filled with stalactites and those that wind through it.

The paintings and petroglyphs that are found within the depths of old caves are examples of prehistoric art that are considered to be masterpieces. These paintings and petroglyphs reveal stories about ancient cultures. Through the process of deciphering the symbolism, capturing the essence of old legends, and experiencing a profound connection with the artistic creations of our distant ancestors, the voyage transforms into an immersive experience.

There are numerous ancient caverns that have functioned as spiritual sanctuaries for a variety of different religions and cultures. As the voyage progresses, it takes the form of a pilgrimage into these holy places, where the chambers are filled with the reverberations of mantras, ceremonies, and other forms of spiritual practice. As a result of the presence of a divine presence in the atmosphere, the journey transforms into a search for spiritual connection and enlightenment.

Temples that have been forgotten: relics of long-lost civilizations

Architectural wonders: The tour continues on to temples that have been forgotten, which are architectural wonders that serve as a tribute to the inventiveness of ancient civilizations. These temples, which have been lost in the folds of time, are embellished with beautiful carvings, towering spires, and sacred geometries that encourage contemplation and awe from visitors.

Historical Narratives: Forgotten temples frequently carry the weight of historical narratives that have been lost from the collective memory of the people. When the voyage is transformed into a historical excavation, the stories of dynasties, religious rituals, and society systems that once flourished within the hallowed walls of these sacred edifices are pieced together.

Cultural Revival: Despite the fact that they have been worn down by the passage of centuries, certain temples that have been forgotten persist as emblems of cultural resistance.

The tour turns into a celebration of the efforts that have been made to resuscitate and conserve these cultural treasures, giving the stones a new lease of life and reviving a sense of appreciation for the heritage that they represent.

The Obstacles and the Benefits of the Trip

Physical Difficulties: The voyage through distant areas, ancient caves, and forgotten temples is not without its share of physical difficulties. As the quest progresses, challenges such as traversing difficult terrains, traveling new paths, and facing the elements become essential components of the experience. The physical challenges, on the other hand, are greeted with a sense of adventure and the excitement of the unknown throughout the process.

A sensitive approach that is rooted in cultural sensitivity is required while exploring distant villages and sacred locations with the intention of preserving their traditions. As a result of the voyage, the journey becomes an exercise in understanding and respecting the traditions and practices of the people encountered along the road, which in turn fosters mutual respect and cultural exchange.

The search for the things that have been forgotten is another objective that falls under the purview of historical preservation programs. The preservation of ancient artifacts, the prevention of vandalism, and the responsible documenting of historical locations are some of the obstacles that must be overcome. Because of this voyage, a promise is made to preserve the history of the past for the generations that will come after us.

Spiritual Reflection: The tour provides opportunities for spiritual reflection as it passes through old caves and temples that have been decommissioned. The difficulties that are encountered become chances for contemplation, meditation, and a profound connection with the spiritual energy that permeates these hallowed areas.

Discovery and Revelation: The journey is full of opportunities for both discovery and revelation at various points along the way. There are further layers of richness added to the narrative as a result of the discovery of hidden items, the decoding of ancient inscriptions, and the gradual revelation of narratives that have been forgotten. Having a great sense of connection with the past is one of the advantages that can be gained from the voyage.

The threads of reverence and exploration are intricately woven together in the fabric of a voyage that takes one through distant regions, ancient caves, and temples that have been forgotten centuries ago.

The journey to find the things that have been lost is more than just a journey through space and time; it is also a journey through culture and spirituality that goes beyond geographical bounds.

There is a story that spans generations that the tourist becomes a part of as they traverse the distant regions, drop into old caves, and stand in wonder before temples that have been forgotten. It is a story about humanity's unending search for connection and understanding, as well as the preservation of the treasures that time has attempted to bury. The echoes of vanished civilizations, the murmurs of spiritual sanctuaries, and the resiliency of forgotten communities form chapters in this story.

All individuals who are interested in discovering the mysteries of the past, treading lightly on the earth, respecting the diversity of civilizations, and standing in wonder before the enduring legacy left by those who came before are invited to participate in this voyage into the forgotten. Following in the footsteps of this search, the globe shows itself to be an infinite reservoir of history and wonder, calling the interested traveler to become not simply an observer but also a custodian of the stories that are concealed in the most isolated nooks, the deepest caves, and the quiet temples of the earth.

Chapter 6

Timeless Connections

When it comes to the broad tapestry that is the human experience, the idea of connections that are timeless overcomes the restrictions of historical borders and cultural disparities. The echoes that reverberate through generations, the braided narratives that transcend different civilizations, and the threads that bind us to the past are all addressed by this. This investigation dives into the intricate web of enduring relationships, examining the ways in which the common experiences, values, and goals of humanity come together to form a fabric that is able to outlast the passage of time.

The Nurturing of the Seeds of Time Through Intergenerational Commitments

The Legacy of the Family The continuity of the family story is the foundation upon which everlasting ties are built. Traditions, memories, and values that are the foundation of an individual's identity are passed down from generation to generation within families. The familial thread is what weaves a tapestry that connects the past, the present, and the future. This can be accomplished through oral histories, heirlooms, or rituals that are performed together.

Ancestral Roots: The concept of ancestral roots encompasses not just the immediate family but also the enduring links that bind people. Getting to know oneself better within the larger framework of historical and cultural narratives can be accomplished through the process of investigating one's genealogy and tracing the beginnings of one's family. The value of ancestral relationships is highlighted by the fact that familial ties have remained strong over the course of time.

Cultural Inheritance: Within the framework of enduring ties, cultural inheritance is an essential component that plays a very important role. In order to promote a sense of continuity that is unaffected by the passage of time, families pass on their languages, customs, and cultural practices to their children. Individuals are connected to a common heritage by cultural threads, which helps to cultivate a collective identity that endures regardless of the passage of time.

The Art and Expression Movement: Bridging the Gap Between Centuries of Creativity

Classical Arts: The sphere of classical arts is a place where timeless linkages are made evident extremely clearly. Whether it be in the realm of music, literature, or visual arts, the works of brilliant artists continue to reverberate throughout the years.

It is possible to develop relationships that transcend the borders of time through the eternal beauty of a symphony, the ageless prose of classic literature, or the brushstrokes on an ancient canvas.

Cultural Narratives Art emerges as a potent medium through which cultural narratives that go back through the ages can be communicated. The transmission of folk tales, epic poetry, and mythological sagas from one generation to the next ultimately results in the creation of a narrative fabric that brings together various cultures. When it comes to art, the presence of shared archetypes and motifs helps to cultivate a universal language that is not constrained by the constraints of time or geography.

Marvels of Architecture Architectural marvels, which serve as a demonstration of human brilliance, create links that span the course of several centuries. Architectural marvels reveal stories of civilizations that have long since vanished, from the architectural splendor of ancient temples to the intricate designs of churches from the middle ages. The aesthetic decisions made during one era frequently reverberate in the creations of subsequent eras, so establishing a conversation that transcends the years.

The pursuit of transcendence through faith as a vehicle for spiritual continuity

Texts of Sacred Importance The sacred texts of a variety of religions provide a powerful expression of the eternal relationships that exist between people. These sacred texts, whether they are the Bible, the Quran, the Vedas, or any other spiritual scriptures, serve as channels through which wisdom and direction are transmitted that are not limited by the constraints of time. Individuals are able to forge a spiritual connection that transcends the constraints of time by drawing sustenance from the everlasting truths that are contained within these works.

Rituals and Ceremonies: Rituals and ceremonies, which have their origins firmly planted in the traditions of various religions, serve to create an everlasting connection between the spiritual and the material worlds. By establishing a connection between individuals and a collective spiritual legacy that transcends millennia, practices that have been handed down from generation to generation produce a shared sense of transcendence.

Iconic Pilgrimage Sites Since pilgrimage sites are revered by people of all different faiths and cultures, they become focal points of connections that will last forever. The footsteps of pilgrims reverberate through the decades, bearing the collective ambitions and devotions of countless individuals who have sought a deeper relationship with the holy. Whether they are in Mecca, Varanasi, or Jerusalem, travelers have traveled back and forth through the ages.

Philosophical Threads: An Investigation into the Knowledge of the Timeless Ages

Philosophical Inquiry Philosophical inquiry, which has been going on for millennia, has been responsible for the emergence of timeless linkages. Questions that have persisted throughout history, such as those concerning existence, morality, and the nature of reality, serve as the threads of contemplation that link earlier thinkers to contemporary philosophers. The quest for knowledge evolves into a collaborative undertaking that is not constrained by the constraints of linear time.

Foundations of Ethics Ethical principles, which originate from the moral reflections of various cultures, result in the creation of a moral tapestry that is enduring over the ages. Over the course of history, the ideas of justice, compassion, and virtue have persisted, and they have played a significant role in the formation of ethical frameworks that direct human behavior and encourage links between individuals and society.

The written word becomes a repository of wisdom that has stood the test of time according to literary wisdom. Classic works of literature, ranging from ancient epics to contemporary philosophical treatises, provide insights into the human condition that continue to be relevant throughout the ages. The investigation of literary wisdom transforms into a voyage through the intellectual history that every human being possesses in common.

Unraveling the Threads of Discovery: The Scientific Continuity of the Investigation

Scientific Inquiry The timeless linkages that exist within the world of science reflect a continuous thread of inquiry that has been going on for quite some time. Each new scientific discovery builds upon the foundations that were established by those who came before it, resulting in the formation of a joint endeavor that is not constrained by the passage of time. Over the course of history, the scientific method functions as a universal language of discovery that has stood the test of time.

Scientific inventions and Discoveries The introduction of new scientific discoveries and inventions can be seen as milestones in the history of human progress. The quest for comprehending the cosmos results in the creation of threads of continuity that link the pioneers of science to contemporary explorers. These threads can be traced back to ancient astronomy and continue into modern space travel. By bridging the gap between different eras and integrating the ideas of innovators from different times, technological breakthroughs become bridges across time.

The understanding of environmental challenges and the need for sustainable practices create a contemporary link to the ecological wisdom of ancient cultures. Therefore, environmental stewardship is an important aspect of environmental protection.

As humanity struggles to come to terms with the effects that its activities have had on the earth, it draws inspiration from indigenous practices that honor the natural environment. These practices have the potential to create timeless connections.

Intergenerational links, creative expression, spiritual continuity, philosophical inquiry, and scientific study are all threads that converge to produce a complex tapestry of human experience. This rich tapestry is created by the intricate weave of timeless connections. A celebration of the oneness that is not limited by the constraints of time or culture is created when we acknowledge the heritage, values, and aspirations that we all share.

In the process of navigating the currents of history, individuals and societies contribute to the continual production of this tapestry, which is a tapestry that depicts the tale of humanity's collective journey through the ages. Exploring timeless connections encourages a sense of shared responsibility for the preservation of cultural legacies, the pursuit of knowledge, and the cultivation of a global ethos that values the richness of our interconnected human experience. This is because the exploration of timeless connections invites reflection on the enduring threads that bind us together. Through the act of embracing this tapestry of humanity, we not only discover a celebration of diversity, but we also find an acknowledgment of the persistent connections that define us over the course of time.

6.1 The protagonist uncovers links between the ancient civilization and present-day cultures

When Dr. Amelia Hartley, an archaeologist who had an intense interest for the wonders of the past, stood in front of the ruins of an ancient civilization, the sun had already sunk beyond the horizon. She had no idea that this excursion would propel her into a journey that would take her beyond the confines of time, revealing linkages between a bygone era and the rich tapestry of civilizations that exist in the present day.

One of the Most Mysterious Discoveries:

The narrative starts out with Dr. Hartley discovering an item that challenged the traditional knowledge of the subject matter. An old civilization that had been lost to the annals of time was hinted at by a relic that has been intricately carved with symbols that are suggestive of an ancient script. During the course of her painstaking excavation of the site, the protagonist's acute eye was able to recognize patterns and themes that had reverberated across history, connecting different cultures that were located on different continents.

Deciphering the Cryptic Code:

Dr. Hartley engaged the assistance of linguists, historians, and anthropologists in order to fulfill his unyielding thirst for knowledge and discover the mysteries that were concealed within the item. The two of them set off on a voyage together with the intention of deciphering the mysterious code that was written in the ancient script. A common language thread that wove through ancient Mesopotamia, Mesoamerica, and beyond was gradually revealed as a result of the hard work performed by the protagonist and the collaborative approach that was taken.

The Threads That Run Through All Continents:

During the course of the protagonist's investigation into the ties between the ancient civilization and the cultures of the current day, a number of unexpected parallels surfaced. As a result of the uncanny similarities that were revealed by rituals, mythologies, and even architectural components, conventional narratives of isolated human development were called into question. Shockwaves were sent through the academic community when it was discovered that these societies shared a common heritage. This understanding prompted a reevaluation of the historical timelines that had previously been constructed.

The Importance of Migration and Trade:

The study of the intertwined history of these civilizations required the identification of important components such as trade routes and migration patterns. Ancient seafaring and overland trade routes that promoted the flow of ideas, technologies, and cultural practices were discovered by Dr. Hartley. These routes were discovered through archaeological excavations. The painstaking investigation conducted by the protagonist provided light on the ways in which migration played a crucial role in the dissemination of information and the shaping of the cultural landscape over the course of several centuries.

Recognizing and Recovering Long-Lost Technologies:

Adding yet more layers to the story was the discovery of ancient technology that were previously believed to have been lost to the passage of time. As a result of Dr. Hartley's exploration, remarkable engineering accomplishments and scientific knowledge were discovered, which contradicted established beliefs about the capabilities of ancient societies. In light of the protagonist's revelations, the timeline of technological advancement was reexamined, and concerns were raised regarding the origins of particular technologies and the spread of those inventions throughout different civilizations.

On the other hand, the resistance to paradigm shifts:

The revelation that ancient civilizations were interconnected was met with opposition from certain segments of the academic community. Those academics who were deeply rooted in conventional perspectives of history were hesitant to accept a paradigm shift that posed a threat to the narratives that had been created.

Due to the fact that she offered strong data that supported the interconnection of various civilizations, Dr. Hartley's trip became not only a quest for knowledge but also a battle against academic lethargy.

Cultural Resilience and Adaptation:

While the protagonist continued her journey of discovery, she came across accounts of cultural resilience and adaptation. The influence of the ancient civilization had not been a one-way street; rather, it demonstrated the adaptability of cultures throughout the course of time. The discoveries made by the protagonist brought to light examples in which contemporary cultures had retained and incorporated historical behaviors, thereby illustrating the significant influence that the past continues to have on the present.

Considerations of Ethical Implications and Adherence to Cultural Values:

Throughout his voyage, Dr. Hartley encountered a number of ethical conundrums. Questions regarding the responsible management of cultural resources were raised as a result of the discovery of sacred sites and artifacts. The protagonist battled with the delicate balance between scientific research and cultural sensitivity, arguing for collaborative techniques that incorporated local populations in the preservation and interpretation of their history.

A Plea for International Cooperation:

As the main character began to put together the complex web that established connections between ancient civilizations and cultures of the current day, she became aware of the importance of international cooperation in the search of knowledge. The narrative eventually developed into a rallying cry for scholars, researchers, and communities all around the world to work together in order to collaboratively investigate and preserve the shared legacy that transcends both geographical and temporal bounds.

The Legacy of the Protagonist's Encounter with the World:

In the closing chapters of the story, the journey of the protagonist culminates in a reimagined comprehension of the course of human history. In the process of developing a new historical paradigm, the connectivity of ancient civilizations and cultures of the current day ended up becoming a cornerstone. A deeper appreciation for the rich tapestry of human history and the interwoven strands that tie us over time and space was nurtured as a result of Dr. Hartley's work, which contributed to the legacy that she also left behind beyond the academic awards she received.

The journey that Dr. Amelia Hartley's discovery of connections between ancient civilizations and cultures of the current day is a demonstration of the transformational power of curiosity and collaborative research.

Creating a captivating tapestry that questions preconceived views of human history, the narrative weaves together elements of archaeology, linguistics, anthropology, and ethical considerations. This results in an engaging tale. At the conclusion of the story, the journey of the protagonist becomes a guiding light, pointing subsequent generations in the direction of a more holistic and integrated knowledge of our common history.

6.2 Flashbacks to historical events that might have influenced the Indus Valley Civilization

Beginning from 3300 BCE and continuing until 1300 BCE, the Indus Valley Civilization flourished along the banks of the Indus River. It is considered to be one of the oldest and most mysterious ancient civilizations. As we continue to explore deeper into the annals of history, we begin to experience flashbacks of key historical events. These events provide us with insights on the potential influences that created the civilization of the Indus Valley. The purpose of this investigation is to take us on a voyage through time, connecting a variety of events that may have left an everlasting impression on the cultural, social, and economic environment of this ancient society.

The Egyptian Connection to Mesopotamia:

A trip back in time to the third millennium before the common era, when the fertile crescent of Mesopotamia was witness to the development of early urban centers such as Sumer was taking place. There is a high probability that the development of writing systems, agricultural advancements, and complicated trading networks in Mesopotamia were significant factors that contributed to the formation of the Indus Valley Civilization. Archaeological evidence reveals that the city-states of Mesopotamia engaged in trade with the Indus Valley, which resulted in cultural exchanges that ended up having a long-lasting impact on both regions.

The Agricultural Revolution of the Neolithic Period:

As we travel further back in time, we come across the Neolithic Agricultural Revolution, a significant event in human history that was responsible for the transition of nomadic lives into permanent agricultural settlements throughout the world. The flashbacks to this revolutionary period reveal the potential influence of early agricultural achievements on the establishment of structured communities along the banks of the Indus River. This is made possible by the fact that the Indus Valley Civilization was founded on agricultural techniques.

The Migration of the Aryans:

Moving forward in time to the second millennium before the common era (BCE), the Aryan migration emerges as an important chapter in our timeline of historical events. There is a possibility that the cultural mosaic that was the Indus Valley Civilization was shaped by the contact between the Indo-Aryans and the local Dravidian inhabitants.

It is possible that the combination of linguistic, theological, and social aspects that occurred during this time period contributed to the formation of the complex identity of the civilization.

A Nexus Between Harappan Culture and Urbanization:

From this point forward, the flashbacks will take us to the urbanization wave that swept across the ancient world, resulting in the establishment of intricate city-states. During this period of unprecedented change, Mesopotamia, Egypt, and the Indus Valley were at the forefront of the transformation. Trade, technological advancement, and cultural exchange all increased in tandem with the growth of urban areas. The flashbacks to this urbanization nexus provide views into the ways in which developments in other regions of the ancient world may have influenced the city planning, infrastructure, and social organization of the civilization that flourished in the Indus Valley.

The Maritime Connections and the Cultures of Seafaring:

Our historical memories shed light on a number of important aspects, one of which is the exceptional seafaring capabilities of ancient civilizations. The interconnection of cultures that engaged in nautical activities, such as the Phoenicians and the Minoans, resulted in the opening of maritime channels that connected the Mediterranean Sea to the Indian Ocean. These nautical networks most certainly made it easier for people to trade products, ideas, and cultural practices, which allowed them to leave their mark on the civilization that flourished in the Indus Valley.

Traditions of the Vedas and Syncretism in Religious Practices:

The Vedic period in ancient India offers yet another glimpse into the past, which may have played a role in shaping the religious and cultural landscape of the Indus Valley Civilization. It is possible that the rich tapestry of religious rituals that can be seen in the archeological remains of the civilization was a result of the combination of Vedic traditions and indigenous beliefs. One possible explanation for the wide variety of deities and rituals that can be found in the archaeological record is that this period of religious syncretism occurred.

Climate Change and Environmental Factors:

In the ancient past, there were climatic upheavals and environmental changes that occurred, and the flashbacks to these events offer a unique viewpoint on the demise of civilizations. As we continue to investigate the interconnection of historical events, it becomes clear that the demise of the Indus Valley Civilization may have been caused by a number of causes, including the alteration of river channels, droughts, and other environmental issues. When we have a better understanding of these ecological flashbacks, we have a better understanding of the intricate web of influences that ancient societies were subject to.

Technological innovations and transfers

Technological flashbacks shed light on the exchange of information and advancements that occurred across different ancient civilizations. The Indus Valley Civilization may have assimilated technological achievements from nearby locations, including techniques for pottery and metallurgy, among other things. The flashbacks to these technical exchanges give light on the dynamic nature of ancient cultures, which were characterized by the free movement of ideas and technologies across geographical boundaries.

Invasion and Conflict:

The ghost of invasion and conflict that plagued the ancient world is also included in the historical flashbacks because of their presence. Even though it had highly developed urban centers, the Indus Valley Civilization was not immune to the influences that came from the outside world. It is possible that the invasion of other civilizations or nomadic nomads was a contributing factor in the ultimate decline of this society, which had previously known great success.

Unraveling the Mysteries and Understanding the Legacy:

As we progress through these historical flashbacks, the legacy of the civilization that flourished in the Indus Valley becomes entwined with the larger tale of human history. The mystery that surrounds the script of the culture, which has not been properly decoded to this day, lends an air of intrigue to our investigation. The process of unraveling the mysteries of the past is a continuing undertaking, and each historical flashback adds a piece to the puzzle. This provides a more nuanced picture of the complex factors that produced the civilization that flourished in the Indus Valley.

A kaleidoscope view of the factors that may have impacted the Indus Valley Civilization is provided via the flashbacks to historical events that are brought up throughout the story. The interconnection of these events gives a vivid picture of the dynamic forces that were at work in the ancient world. These events include cultural exchanges, trade networks, and climate shifts, as well as the transfer of technological knowledge. During the course of our exploration of these historical flashbacks, we not only acquire a more profound comprehension of the past, but we also acquire a more comprehensive grasp of the tangled web that is human society. Recognizing that the past is a mosaic of interrelated events that impact both our present and our future, the echoes that travel through time encourage us to continue our exploration.

6.3 Unravel the connection between the lost language and modern languages

The chronicles of linguistic history are embellished with the vestiges of languages that have been lost, old tongues that once reverberated through the ages when they were spoken. There are intricate threads that join the past and the present, and when we go on a journey to uncover the connection between these vanished languages and modern linguistic landscapes, we realize that we are investigating these connections. The cuneiform inscriptions of Akkadian, the hieroglyphs of Ancient Egypt, and the cryptic symbols of the Indus Valley are just few of the lost languages that contain clues to the development of human communication and its lasting influence on the languages that are spoken today.

Keeping the Reverberations of the Past Within Us:

The maintenance of written records becomes an essential beginning point in the process of determining the connection between languages that have been lost and those that are now spoken. Archaeologists and linguists have invested a great deal of time and effort into decoding ancient writings, which has resulted in the dissemination of important information. An example of this would be the Rosetta Stone, which was used as a key to uncover the mysteries of Egyptian hieroglyphs. This stone served as a bridge between the ancient world and our modern knowledge of language.

Unlocking the Secrets of the Akkadian Legacy:

It was originally the lingua franca of the ancient Near East, and the Akkadian language, which was written in cuneiform script on clay tablets, represented that language. It is becoming increasingly clear that there is a connection to contemporary Semitic languages as we continue to understand it. An indelible mark was left on the formation of languages such as Hebrew, Aramaic, and Arabic as a result of the influence of Akkadian, which reverberates down the corridors of time. Through the process of deciphering Akkadian tablets, we are able to trace linguistic continuity that spans over a period of millennia.

In the role as time capsules, hieroglyphs are:

It is a monument to the lasting power of written language that the hieroglyphic alphabet of ancient Egypt, which was engraved onto the walls of temples and the graves of royal families, has survived. A window into the linguistic legacy of ancient Egypt was opened as a result of the efforts that were made to decode hieroglyphs, which culminated in the breakthrough work that was done by Jean-Francois Champollion. There is a connection between hieroglyphs and modern languages not only in the process of deciphering them, but also in the recognition of linguistic borrowings and influences that have made their way into the ever-changing landscape of language.

Indus Script: The Unyielding Mystery:

The mystery that surrounds the script of the ancient civilization that flourished in the Indus Valley presents an additional layer of difficulty to our investigation. Historiographers and linguists alike are fascinated by the script, which has not yet been decoded. As our investigation into the relationship between the Indus script and contemporary languages continues, we come across a plethora of hypotheses and assumptions around the topic. Others imply a more complicated linguistic scenario, while others claim a relationship to Dravidian languages as the possible explanation. In addition to serving as a reminder that certain linguistic connections continue to be elusive, the enigma surrounding the Indus script also acts as an invitation for more investigation and discovery.

Regarding the Isolation of Languages and Their Genetic Connections:

The idea of linguistic isolation and the genetic ties between languages becomes extremely important as we work toward our goal of determining the connection between modern languages and languages that have been lost. Not all ancient languages are related to one another in any obvious way, and some of them live in isolation. Some of these languages, such as Latin, have developed into the Romance languages that are spoken today. An understanding of the ways in which linguistic evolution has produced the unique fabric of current languages can be gained through comprehension of the genetic links that exist across languages.

The Latin Language's Living Heritage:

In the shape of the Romance languages, Latin, which was once the language of the Roman Empire, has left behind a legacy that will endure for generations to come. It is possible to trace the origins of the languages of Spain, France, Italy, Portugal, and Romania all back to Latin. The relationship between Latin and the Romance languages is not only historical; rather, it continues to be present in the lexicon, syntax, and even sound of these contemporary languages. The classical world and the Romance-speaking nations of today are connected by the use of Latin, which acts as a language bridge that transcends millennia.

Language Contact and Borrowing:

One of the dynamic forces that shapes the evolution of language is the interaction between languages, which occurs through contact and borrowing one another. The phenomena of language contact is becoming more obvious as we explore the connection between languages that have been lost and those that are currently spoken. The Silk Road, old trade routes, and cultural interactions have all played a role in facilitating the borrowing of words, idioms, and even grammatical structures from one language to another. The richness and diversity of modern languages can be attributed, in part, to the process of cross-pollination.

Linguistic Fusion: Pidgins and Creoles

The evolution of pidgins and creoles offers an additional perspective from which to investigate the relationship between languages that have been lost and the advancements that have been made in modern language. Pidgins, which are simplified languages that emerge as a result of conversations between people, frequently combine aspects from more than one language. Creoles are languages that develop into fully developed languages after being born from pidgins in communities that are stable. The linguistic aspects that are combined in creoles and pidgins are a reflection of the fluidity and adaptability of language. They demonstrate how different linguistic influences can come together to generate new and exciting forms of communication.

Reviving Languages from the Past:

The revitalization of ancient languages, which were until recently thought to be dormant, brings an interesting new facet to our investigation. Hebrew, for instance, went through a period of revitalization as a spoken language in the latter half of the 19th century and the early 20th century. There is a strong and everlasting connection between the past and the present, which is highlighted by the efforts that are being made to bring old languages back to life, whether for cultural, religious, or intellectual purposes. These revival initiatives are important in ensuring the continuation of linguistic traditions and contributing to their preservation.

Computational linguistics and digital tools:

At this point in time, digital tools and computational linguistics provide novel approaches to the problem of determining the relationship between languages that have been lost and those that are currently in use. The study of linguistic data is made easier by the use of sophisticated algorithms and machine learning techniques. This makes it possible to interpret ancient scripts and investigate the connections between different languages. The convergence of technology and linguistics paves the way for the exploration of new territories in our pursuit of an understanding of the development of language.

This is a monument to the resiliency and adaptability of human communication, as we come to the end of our voyage through the intricate fabric of linguistic history. The connection between languages that have been lost and languages that are used now emerges on this journey. A piece of the puzzle that connects the threads of the past to the linguistic tapestry of today is held by each linguistic relic. This includes the deciphered scripts of Akkadian and hieroglyphs, as well as the mysterious Indus script. The study of lost languages is not only an exercise in historical linguistics; rather, it is an intriguing investigation into the enduring echoes that resonate over time, thereby influencing the way in which we talk and see the world. Language, like a river, carries with it the sediment of ages past, leaving an indelible mark on the landscapes of our common human experience. This is something that we have discovered in our constant search to uncover the linguistic conundrum.

6.4 Discovery of a hidden chamber with artifacts hinting at advanced technology

An unanticipated discovery was made by a group of courageous researchers when they were exploring the sacred corridors of an ancient archaeological site. They discovered a hidden room that had been buried for generations, with its secrets being sealed away in the embrace of time." The contents of the room, which contained objects that indicated a degree of technological skill that was previously thought to be inconceivable for the era, would present a challenge to the dominant narratives established about the past. This story develops as we investigate the exciting discovery of a hidden chamber and the treasures that are contained within it. It provides us with glimpses into a past that contradicts our preconceived views about something.

The Odyssey of Archaeological Discovery:

In the beginning of the game, a group of archaeologists set out to conduct an excavation in a spot that is rich in history. This location was previously believed to have divulged all of its secrets. On the other hand, new developments in technology, such as ground-penetrating radar and LiDAR, provided hints about anomalies that existed beneath the surface, which increased the researchers' level of curiosity. An archeological expedition was undertaken by the group, which was equipped with these cutting-edge tools. Their objective was to discover the mysteries that were concealed beneath the layers of soil and time.

Unveiling the Secret Section of the Building:

It was when the team identified some small abnormalities in the architectural layout of the site that they made their breakthrough. As ground-penetrating radar proved the existence of a hidden chamber, a buried area that had avoided detection for generations, the atmosphere was filled with excitement. The archaeologists diligently dug the area, and while they did so, they discovered a blocked door that was decorated with exquisite carvings and symbols, which suggested the significance of what was located beyond.

Technological marvels: the artifacts that are included within:

As soon as the researchers entered the concealed chamber, they were greeted by a spectacular sight: a treasure trove of artifacts that defied the technological norms that were believed to be prevalent throughout the time period to which the site was attributed. Among the discoveries were complex mechanisms that resembled gear systems, carefully constructed tools with precision that exceeded the capabilities that were known at the time, and mysterious devices that were ornamented with symbols that hinted at a deep understanding of science and engineering.

In the context of time, the anomaly is as follows:

Taking into consideration the chronological context of the archaeological site, the artifacts that were found within the concealed room presented a puzzling anomaly. Despite the fact that radiocarbon dating and stratigraphic research initially suggested an age that was consistent with the structures that were located in the surrounding area, the technological sophistication of the items that were discovered appeared to be beyond the capabilities that were thought to be accessible to the ancient civilization. The researchers were left struggling with concerns that did not have straightforward solutions as a result of the juxtaposition of cutting-edge technology within an environment that appeared to be somewhat ancient.

Having a New Perspective on the Development of Technology:

The revelation sparked a reassessment of the conventional narrative of the march of technological advancement. A level of technological ingenuity that challenged the linear trajectory that is typically associated with human development was hinted at by the artifacts through their presence. Is it possible that the ancient civilization had achieved great heights of scientific prowess, only to have those achievements buried beneath the sands of time instead? In an effort to decipher the secrets that were contained inside the artifacts, the scholars, who were now entangled in a web of supposition and inquiry, decided to investigate.

Using the Past to Reverse Engineer the Present:

A significant amount of attention and investigation was directed toward the objects that were found within the concealed room. Together, groups of specialists from a wide variety of disciplines, spanning from engineering to archaeology, worked together to figure out what the mysterious gadgets were and how they worked exactly. For the purpose of gaining an understanding of the inner workings of the technical marvels that were in front of them, the procedure included painstaking recording, scanning in three dimensions, and even attempts at reverse engineering.

Theories Regarding the Influence of Extraterrestrial Beings:

There was a proliferation of speculation and speculations as the news of the find spread, one of which was the intriguing notion that the artifacts suggested the presence of extraterrestrial influence. Conjecture that ancient civilizations may have had interactions with entities or powers beyond Earth was fostered by the meticulous accuracy and advanced design of the gadgets, which inspired technological breakthroughs that were beyond the knowledge of their contemporaries for the time.

The Cultural and Social Consequences of the Situation:

Beyond the realms of archaeology and technology, the consequences of the finding were far-reaching.

Based on the artifacts, it was possible to infer that the culture in issue possessed knowledge and capacities that were significantly greater than what had been established in the past. The potential of an ancient civilization that was technologically advanced posed a challenge to the conventional ideas that have been held about the progression of society. It also brought up problems regarding the transmission of information, the presence of cultures that have been lost, and the durability of human creativity over the course of time.

Ethical Considerations and the Preservation of the Environment:

Ethical considerations about the preservation and sharing of the findings were brought to light as a result of the reveal of the subterranean room. The objects were not only archeological curiosities; rather, they had the potential to provide windows into a hidden chapter in the history of humanity. It became a delicate dance to strike a balance between the desire to disseminate information and the necessity to conserve the site and its relics. This required collaboration between scholars, historians, and preservation professionals.

The narrative that is not yet complete:

Despite the fact that the researchers continued to probe further into the mysteries of the subterranean chamber, the tale remained unfinished, with more questions than answers. The artifacts provided evidence of a level of technological competence that posed a challenge to the standard timeframes and narratives on the progression of cultural evolution. Both the dynamic character of archaeological investigation and the ever-evolving understanding of our common human past were brought to light by the continuous efforts to comprehend the repercussions of the discovery.

It is a monument to the boundless possibilities that lie beneath the surface of our archaeological past that the discovery of a hidden chamber that contained items that hinted at high technology was made. The items contained within present us with the challenge of reevaluating our preconceived assumptions regarding the progression of technology, the development of culture, and the tenacity of human creativity over the course of time. Our understanding of the past is a tapestry that is woven with strands of discovery, speculation, and the unrelenting desire of knowledge. As scholars continue to unravel the riddles stored inside the hidden chamber, the story becomes a poignant reminder that this is the case. The secret chamber pulls us, asking us to investigate the mystery that lies within and to broaden our understanding of the extensive and intricate past that comes together to form our shared heritage.

Chapter 7

Unveiling the Enigma

In the field of archaeology, the boundaries of our understanding of the past are continually being pushed further and further. The concept of secret chambers that conceal objects that contradict accepted narratives is one that possesses an innate attraction. This adventure sets out on an enthralling voyage, during which it will navigate the findings of hidden rooms and solve archeological mysteries that contradict conventional thinking. It will also provide glimpses into previous civilizations that have been veiled by the passage of time.

The Odyssey of Archaeological Discovery:

The narrative starts off with the daring endeavors of archaeologists who are equipped with the most advanced technologies. Both ground-penetrating radar and LiDAR are considered to be treasure maps of the modern day since they identify anomalies that lurk beneath the surface. The technologies that are used in contemporary archaeology make it possible for researchers to locate secret chambers that were previously missed by the methods that were used in the past. As these anomalies raise the chance that there are hidden mysteries that are just waiting to be discovered, the excitement level continues to rise.

Revealing the Hidden room: The breakthrough occurs when painstaking excavation reveals the entrance to a room that has been forgotten for a very long time and is decorated with elaborate carvings and symbols. As the story progresses, symbolism frequently provides hints about the significance of what is hidden behind the closed entrance, which lends an air of mystique to the ongoing narrative. When the room is finally shown, the anticipation is replaced by a spectacular sight: a treasure trove of relics that contradicts the technological conventions that were believed to be prevalent during the presumed age.

Technological marvels: the artifacts that are included within:

The concealed chamber is not merely a location that has been preserved in time; rather, it is a treasure trove of relics that contradict the conventional wisdom.

Among the discoveries are mechanisms that resemble advanced gear systems, tools that demonstrate precision that is beyond the capabilities that were recognized at the time, and gadgets that are ornamented with symbols that hint at a deep understanding of physics and engineering. The discovery of these artifacts not only rewrites the history of the civilization in question, but it also prompts a reevaluation of the path that technological growth took in the ancient world.

An Anomaly in the Temporal Context The artifacts present a contradiction, which can be seen as an anomaly in the context of time that the archeological site is situated in. Initial dating methods indicate an age that is consistent with the structures that are located in the surrounding area; yet, the technological sophistication shows that the ancient civilization possessed capabilities that were above what was thought to be possible of them. Scholars are prompted to examine established timeframes as a result of this incongruity, which leads to an intriguing investigation into whether or not the culture in question reached peaks of technological capability that have been lost to history.

A Reconsideration of the Linear Narrative of technical Progress The discovery promotes a rethinking of the linear narrative of technical progression. Were there fluctuations in the development of historical civilizations that contradicted our preconceived notions, such as peaks and valleys? The items that are found within the concealed chamber present us with a challenge to reimagine the path that technological evolution has taken. They point to the possibility that certain ancient cultures may have achieved levels of sophistication that were significantly higher than what was previously assumed.

The artifacts become the focal point of an interdisciplinary partnership, with archaeologists and engineers working together to determine the purpose and functionality of the artifacts. This is described as "reverse engineering the past." An understanding of the inner workings of these technological wonders can be gained through the use of meticulous documentation, scanning in three dimensions, and attempts at reverse engineering. Unlocking the secrets that are inscribed in the artifacts is the goal of the collaborative efforts that are being made to bridge the gap between the past and the recent past.

Theories Regarding the Influence of Extraterrestrial Beings:

As the word of the discovery travels, there is a great deal of speculation. Because of the complexity of the artifacts, theories have been proposed that claim ancient civilizations were influenced by extraterrestrial beings. One alternate explanation for the technological prowess that is hinted at within the hidden chamber is the tempting concept that advanced knowledge may have been given onto ancient nations by creatures from beyond Earth. This idea grabs the imagination and offers an alternative explanation for advanced technology.

Cultural and societal ramifications: Beyond the technological marvels, the finding has enormous cultural and societal ramifications. It challenges established beliefs about the capabilities of ancient societies, so raising issues about the transfer of information, the presence of cultures that may have been lost, and the persistence of human creativity over the course of time. The narrative goes beyond the area of archaeology and touches on the broader implications for comprehending the evolution of human societies to become more comprehensive.

Ethical Considerations and the Preservation of the Environment:

There are ethical problems that arise as a result of the discovery of the subterranean room. These objects are not merely interesting to look at; rather, they are windows into a previously untold chapter in the history of humanity. Establishing a delicate equilibrium between the desire to share knowledge and the necessity to conserve the site and the artifacts that it contains becomes a challenging undertaking. An examination of the ethical implications of archaeological finds is presented in the tale, with an emphasis placed on the significance of the responsible preservation and transmission of newly discovered information.

The Unfinished story: As the investigators continue to probe deeper into the mysteries of the hidden chamber, the story continues to be unfinished. The artifacts provide evidence of a level of technological proficiency that calls into question the timelines and narratives that are typically used. Both the dynamic character of archaeological investigation and the ever-evolving understanding of our common human past are highlighted by the continuous efforts that are being made to comprehend the repercussions of the discovery. With its mysterious relics, the hidden chamber continues to beckon, extending an invitation for deeper exploration and enhancing our understanding of the rich and complicated past that binds us all together.

In the broad fabric of human history, the discovery of a hidden room containing artifacts that hint at high technology stands as a monument to the inexhaustible mysteries that are waiting to be revealed after years of speculation. The voyage through this narrative is a reflection of the continual pursuit of knowledge in archaeology, which involves an unending study of secret regions that challenge our understanding of the past. The hidden chamber is not merely a physical location; rather, it is a gateway to the mystery of ancient civilizations and a bridge to reimagining the complexity of human creativity and inventiveness throughout the ages.

7.1 Climax: Confrontation with the secret society and decoding the final piece of the puzzle

In the climax of our story, the heroes find themselves on the verge of a confrontation with a secret society that operates in the shadows. This society is the mastermind behind the mystery that has been the driving force behind the plot. As the level of suspense reaches its highest point, the last piece of the puzzle, which is cloaked in mystery, is waiting to be deciphered. Not only does this climax moment alleviate the tension in the narrative, but it also discloses the actual depth of the mystery that has fascinated both our protagonists and the readers.

The Building Storm: The story methodically prepares the audience for the climax by establishing a sense of the imminent conflict that is about to take place. As the novel progresses, our characters are led to the doorstep of the secret organization by a series of clues and discoveries that have been accumulated throughout the narrative. The group that was formerly difficult to find and that was functioning in the shadows is now in the spotlight.

At this point, the hidden objective that has been driving the plot up until this point is on the approach of being revealed.

The characters have been relentlessly searching for the breadcrumbs that were left behind by the secret society. They have been motivated by a combination of curiosity, tenacity, and a sense of duty at the same time. They have made a number of discoveries, ranging from historic documents to secret communications, and each one has led them closer to the core of the enigma. As they get ready to meet the people who are responsible for the mystery, the tension rises, and the reader is left on the tip of their seat, anxious to see how the mystery is solved.

During the confrontation with the hidden society, a moment of discovery and reckoning occurs. This is the second part of the story series. When the heroes finally face the mysterious individuals who are responsible for the intricate puzzle, they are armed with the knowledge that they have gained throughout their arduous journey. It is possible that the scene is an ancient chamber or a secret gathering spot, as it is cloaked in darkness and filled with a palpable feeling of mystery due to the fact that it is surrounded by shadows.

When this crucial moment occurred, it became clear that the leaders of the secret society are not merely adversaries but rather individuals who are driven by their own personal convictions and objectives. The conversation that they have with the protagonists reveals the true nature of their aims and the historical significance of the mystery. This conversation tears away the layers of secrecy that have been surrounding the mystery. In order to comprehend the intricate interplay of motivations that has resulted in this final showdown, the reader is given the opportunity to enter the thoughts of both of the parties involved.

Deciphering the Final Piece: As the verbal encounter progresses, the protagonists gain knowledge of the final piece of the jigsaw, which is the linchpin that draws together the other components of the mystery. It may be an old artifact, a hidden location, or a revelation that questions the fundamental foundation of the protagonists' perception of the world. All of these things are all possibilities.

However, the process of decoding is not quite as simple as it may seem. Because of this, it is necessary for the characters to make use of the information that they have gathered along their adventure. For the purpose of deciphering the mysteries that are included within the final piece, it is necessary to decipher cryptic symbols, old languages, and arcane references. Due to the fact that the objectives of the secret society are on the verge of being realized, the level of anxiety increases as time becomes an increasingly important component.

The Revelation: The moment of revelation is a literary peak; it is the climax of the major enigma that the story is trying to convey. During the process of deciphering the final piece, the characters experience a wave of realizations that wash over them. A storyline that spans millennia and connects diverse pieces in a magnificent tapestry of history, science, and human aspiration is beginning to take shape, and the riddle, which was previously a mosaic of disjointed fragments, is beginning to transform into a coherent narrative.

Not only does the revelation provide answers to problems, but it also presents new questions, broadening the scope of the narrative. It drives the protagonists to confront the ramifications of the obtained knowledge and challenges the ideas that they have about the outcome of the story. There is a surge of comprehension that occurs for the reader as well, as they observe the components of the narrative coming together with the pleasant click of a puzzle that has been carefully handcrafted.

Deciphering Motivations: At the same time that the decoding process is taking place, the motivations of both the protagonists and the secret society are being investigated. At first glance, the disagreement appeared to be basic; yet, it has now shown multiple layers of intricacy. At the same time as the aims of the secret society, which were previously veiled in ambiguity, are revealed, the characters are forced to deal with the ramifications of their findings.

The quest of knowledge, the desire for power, or a mission that is built in a perceived duty to protect or influence the course of history are all examples of motivations that might drive people to act in certain ways. The climax functions as a psychological battleground, representing a situation in which the conflict of principles is just as powerful as any physical confrontation. Having reached their maximum potential in terms of their complexity, the characters now traverse the moral and ethical ramifications of the decisions they make.

Battle and Resolution: The battle with the secret society achieves its pinnacle when the protagonists and antagonists come face to face in a dramatic confrontation that is the culmination of the story. The battlefield is not simply a physical one; it is both intellectual and emotional. The setting could be an ancient temple, a secret cavern, or the midst of a bustling city, but the combat is not just physical.

The resolution of the issue involves a number of different paths. While there is a possibility that physical confrontations could take place, the actual climax will be the resolving of the underlying mystery. It is up to the heroes to determine how they will put the knowledge they have acquired to use. What are the chances that they will be able to foil the schemes of the secret society, expose the truth to the world, or build an unforeseen partnership that goes beyond the conflict?

The narrative then enters the denouement, which is a phase of resolution, reflection, and closure, as the climax begins to fade away until it reaches its conclusion. The consequences of the clash have repercussions that are felt throughout the lives of the people and the world that they inhabit. As the story progresses, loose ends are resolved, and the repercussions of the protagonists' decisions become crystal clear.

In addition, the denouement affords the characters the chance to contemplate the voyage they have had up until this point. Throughout the course of the story, various themes are introduced, and they eventually come to the forefront. Some of these themes include the nature of power, the implications of knowledge, and the resiliency of the human spirit. After the reader has successfully navigated the twists and turns of the story and observed the metamorphosis of the protagonists, they are left with a sense of catharsis during the conclusion of the story.

The climax, which includes the encounter with the secret organization and the deciphering of the final piece of the puzzle, is the peak of the narrative. It is the culmination of tension, revelation, and resolve. The reader is carried on a rollercoaster of emotions as the protagonist's struggle to come to terms with the ramifications of their discoveries. These emotions range from amazement and catharsis to tension and anticipation. The mystery that has been driving the story forward is finally revealed at this climactic point, and it leaves an unforgettable mark on the reader's mind. Following its ascent through the peaks of mystery and revelation, the narrative is now descending into the denouement, which is where the consequences of the choices made by the characters reverberate throughout the latter pages of the book.

7.2 Revelation of the civilization's purpose and the reason behind its disappearance

As one travels through the winding passageways of history, there are certain civilizations that are veiled in mystery. These civilizations have left behind mysterious remnants that are begging to be understood. The heroes are getting closer and closer to the core of the mystery as our story progresses. They are discovering the reason behind the origin of the ancient civilization as well as the enigmatic mystery surrounding its disappearance. The objective of this investigation is to uncover the complexities of the civilization's mission and the mysterious reasons behind its disappearance. This investigation goes into the disclosures that redefine the very essence of civilization.

Investigating the Purpose: As the protagonists work their way through the pieces of the history of the civilization, a momentous revelation comes to light: the purpose that drove the ancient society onward. Regardless of whether it is a cosmic quest for knowledge, the pursuit of spiritual enlightenment, or a pragmatic mission to harness the resources of the natural world, the goal of civilization becomes a guiding light that illuminates the motivations behind its enormous achievements.

There is a possibility that the story will reveal the presence of a long-forgotten order that is devoted to the preservation of information or a utopian society that is working toward achieving harmony with the environment. Through the accomplishments of the civilization, the purpose is like a hidden thread that weaves through the fabric of the achievements. It provides the characters and the readers with a glimpse into the hopes and desires that were the driving force behind this forgotten society.

The Nexus of Knowledge and Power The revelation of the goal of the civilization is frequently intertwined with the nexus of knowledge and power. Perhaps the civilization's goal was to discover the mysteries of the cosmos and harness the power of the cosmos in order to bring its people to levels of knowledge and influence that had never been seen before. This search of knowledge may have resulted in technological marvels, esoteric insight, or a mastery of arts and sciences that distinguished the culture from others.

On the other hand, the story also investigates the moral repercussions that come with having such extraordinary power. Did the search of knowledge by the civilization unintentionally plant the seeds that would eventually lead to its demise? A thematic crucible is created at the confluence of knowledge and power, where the heroes are forced to contend with the repercussions of discovering old knowledge that questions the very foundation of their current thinking.

Spiritual Enlightenment and Ritualistic activities: Another aspect of the civilization's aim may revolve around spiritual enlightenment and ritualistic activities. This is the third and last point. There is a possibility that the ancient society set out on a journey of transcendence, with the intention of establishing a more profound relationship with the divine or the cosmos. The rituals, ceremonies, and sacred knowledge that characterized the spiritual journey of the civilization form an essential component in one's comprehension of the goal of the civilization.

During the process of deciphering these features, the protagonists can discover that they are caught up in a complex web of old beliefs, symbolic languages, and metaphysical ideas. The protagonists are forced to confront the fundamental truths that are inscribed in the spiritual practices of the civilization that has since perished, which causes the tale to morph into a mystical trip.

Ecological Harmony and Resource Management: The goal of some ancient societies was inextricably linked to the management of resources and the maintenance of ecological harmony.

It is possible that the civilization had perfected sustainable methods, lived in harmony with the natural environment, and constructed architectural marvels that blended in perfectly with their surroundings. The disclosure of such an environmentally focused aim poses a challenge to the dominant ideas of progress and sustainability in the modern world.

While the heroes are discovering the brilliant methods that the civilization uses to manage its resources, they are also struggling with the ramifications that these approaches have for their own society. The narrative evolves into a contemplation on the precarious equilibrium that exists between human advancement and environmental stewardship, resonating with the teachings of a civilization that has been lost to the passage of time.

Unraveling the Mystery of the Disappearance:

No matter how profound the revelation of the civilization's purpose may be, it will invariably be overshadowed by the mystery of the civilization's absence. The narrative then shifts its focus to investigate the mysterious factors that led to the collapse of the civilization. Did it happen as a result of a catastrophic incident, a slow decline, or a conscious decision to retreat from the stage of history?

As the story progresses, the characters embark on a twofold journey: first, they uncover the mysteries surrounding the purpose of the civilization, and then they piece together the evidence that led to its disappearance. There is a possibility that they will be able to navigate through deserted towns, interpret encrypted inscriptions, and comprehend old warnings that describe the imminent danger. The disappearance becomes a puzzle within a puzzle, which adds another layer of complexity to the story.

Catastrophic Occurrences and Natural Disasters:

Catastrophic events or natural disasters that swept through the civilization and erased it off the map could be one of the conceivable reasons for the demise of the civilization. The story investigates the relics of old catastrophe mitigation systems, warnings engraved into stone, or the remnants of a society that is struggling to cope with the forces of nature that are beyond its control.

There is a possibility that the protagonists would discover proof of seismic activity, climate change, or celestial occurrences that contributed to the destruction of civilization. The story presents a vivid image of a community that is struggling to come to terms with its fragility in the face of the uncontrollable forces that ultimately led to its demise.

Decay of Society and Strife Within the Individual:

There is a possibility that the ancient society was plagued by intrigue and internal warfare, which ultimately led to the ruin of its foundations and a gradual but unstoppable decline throughout its history. In this narrative, the layers of societal institutions, political maneuverings, and individual conflicts that were the seeds of the civilization's death from within are peeled back one by one.

The heroes are confronted with the sobering fact that even the most evolved civilizations are susceptible to the seeds of their own doom as they unearth the echoes of a society that was once lively but is now plagued by decadence and internal power struggles.

The pursuit of knowledge and technology advancement, while done with the best of intentions, can occasionally result in the release of unexpected consequences. This is referred to as technical hubris. The story investigates the idea that the civilization, in its pursuit of dominance over the natural world, may have violated ethical boundaries or interacted with forces that were beyond its means of comprehension.

As a result of the reveal of technological arrogance and unforeseen repercussions, the story becomes a cautionary tale, which prompts the protagonists to contemplate the possible hazards of unfettered progress as well as the ethical duties that come along with the gain of superior knowledge.

Cultural Transformation and Integration: An original viewpoint on the extinction of civilization could involve the deliberate undertaking of cultural transformation and the incorporation of surrounding societies. The story reveals evidence of diplomatic attempts, cultural exchange, and even the deliberate spread of the civilization's knowledge and people in order to ensure that its legacy will continue to live on in the fabric of other cultures.

The characters struggle with issues of identity and continuity as they endeavor to piece together this narrative of planned transformation. Additionally, they are confronted with the far-reaching impact that the intentional breakdown of a civilization can have.

The revelation of the civilization's mission and the mystery surrounding its disappearance become the two pillars that sustain the conclusion of the narrative. Characters are left to struggle with the enigmatic mystery of the old society's disappearance, despite the fact that they now possess profound insights into the factors that played a role in shaping the ancient society.

The reader, having successfully negotiated the maze of discoveries and mysteries, is left with a sense of awe and contemplation, considering the lessons and reflections hidden in the rise and fall of a civilization that has been lost to the passage of time. The narrative echoes the timeless reality that the secrets of the past continue to shape the present and enlighten the route forward as the characters and readers alike confront the duality of purpose and disappearance over the course of the story.

7.3 Reflection on the implications of the discovered knowledge on modern society

The echoes of the past ricochet into the present as the characters of our story explore the mysteries of an ancient civilization, deciphering its purpose and the reasons behind its disappearance so that they can understand why it vanished. The tremendous effects that the newly acquired information has on contemporary society are investigated in depth by this investigation. In the process of altering viewpoints and challenging preconceptions, the disclosures, which are embedded in the relics of a mysterious past, become a lens through which the characters and the readers alike reflect on the complexities of current reality.

The Wisdom of Technology and the Responsibility to Practice Ethics:

The pursuit of knowledge and technological prowess by the ancient civilization provides a perspective on modern society that is both paradoxical and illuminating. As we read the story, we are encouraged to think about the repercussions that come with using sophisticated technologies in a responsible manner. In the process of deciphering the accomplishments of the ancient society, the characters confront the question of how contemporary society manages to strike a balance between the pursuit of innovation and ethical duty.

In the course of the story, a cautionary tale is told, which recommends that modern civilization proceed with caution when it comes to the progress of scientific knowledge. As a mirror, the ancient society, with its technological arrogance, acts as a reflection, pushing us to contemplate the unexpected repercussions and ethical implications of our own scientific achievements.

Environmental Stewardship and Sustainability: If the newly discovered information reveals that a historical society was intimately sensitive to ecological harmony and resource management, then the story becomes a rallying cry for contemporary society to take action. As we see the protagonist's struggle to come to terms with the repercussions of the civilization's eco-centric goal, we are prompted to contemplate the urgent requirement for responsibility toward the environment.

The ancient society becomes both a cautionary story and an inspiration in light of the fact that climate change and diminishing resources are having an impact on the world.

The story encourages us to reconsider our connection to the natural world and promotes the adoption of environmentally responsible behaviors that are reminiscent of the sage advice of a civilization that once flourished in harmony with our natural surroundings.

The Decay of Society and Strife Within the Individual:

The revelation of internal warfare and societal disintegration within the ancient civilization prompts a melancholy reflection on the precarious nature of the structures that make up societies. The narrative serves as a powerful warning that even the most advanced cultures can fall prey to the corrosive forces of decadence and internal conflict—a fact that is brought home by the narrative.

The contemporary society, which is characterized by its own socio economic issues, political strife, and ethical conundrums, is currently at a decisive juncture. The collapse of the ancient civilization serves as a cautionary tale, prompting us to investigate the causes of the problems that plague contemporary society and to work toward the development of a social fabric that is both durable and welcoming to all.

Cultural Integration and Diversity: If the story is told in a way that reveals a story of cultural transformation and integration that was done on purpose, then the story becomes a reflection on the richness of diversity. We are prompted to examine the transformational power of cultural interchange as a result of the characters' investigation of the deliberate dissemination of knowledge and people.

In today's increasingly interconnected world, the deliberate breakdown of an old civilization can be interpreted as a metaphor for the possibility for different civilizations to complement and build upon one another. The story encourages contemporary society to embrace cultural integration, with the goal of cultivating an atmosphere in which diversity is not only accepted but celebrated.

Education and the Transfer of Knowledge The ancient civilization's quest for knowledge serves as a guiding light that sheds light on the significance of education and the transfer of knowledge. The story compels us to contemplate the enduring impact of a culture that placed a high value on the gathering and diffusion of knowledge from generation to generation.

Within the context of the modern era, the ramifications extend to educational systems as well as the availability of available information. In order to ensure that the lessons learned from the past are not lost to the sands of time, the story encourages us to make education a priority as a means of empowering both individuals and societies.

Striking a Balance Between Tradition and Progress The revealed wisdom, which is deeply rooted in the goal of the ancient civilization, compels one to reflect on the delicate balance that exists between tradition and progress. The narrative evolves into a meditation on the pursuit of development in contemporary society as the characters make their way through the ruins of a society that achieved incredible heights while remaining firmly rooted in its traditions.

The teaching is subtle; it is a call for advancement that does not throw away the knowledge that tradition has to offer. The protagonists, who are situated at the point where the past and the present meet, encourage us to contemplate the ways in which contemporary society might construct a way forward that incorporates innovation with the values that have stood the test of time and are the foundation of human civilization.

Making Ethical Decisions in the Face of Power The ancient civilization's goal served as a moral crucible for modern society, and the nexus of knowledge and power in that purpose plays a role in the decision-making process. The story develops moral conundrums, which force the protagonists and the readers alike to confront the repercussions of engaging in activities that include the use of power and influence.

It is a story that encourages society to engage in ethical decision-making in a world where technology breakthroughs provide unparalleled power. It also emphasizes the necessity of having checks and balances in place to prevent the misuse of knowledge and authority.

Lessons Learned from Catastrophic Occurrences If the story is told in the form of a story about a series of catastrophic occurrences that led to the extinction of an ancient civilization, then the story transforms into a profound meditation on the unpredictability of the future. We are prompted to contemplate our own vulnerabilities in the face of natural disasters, pandemics, or other unforeseen global calamities as we are confronted by the protagonists, who are confronting the remnants of a society that has been brought down by forces that are beyond its control.

An old society serves as a metaphor for the resiliency that is necessary in the present period. This metaphor highlights the significance of being prepared, working together, and being able to adapt in order to successfully navigate an unpredictable future.

Legacy and Continuity: As the story comes to a close, the protagonists and the audience both find themselves at a crossroads where legacy and continuity intersect. The consequences of the newly revealed information are not limited to the bounds of the ancient civilization; rather, they reverberate well into the present and the future of contemporary world society.

We are prompted to contemplate the legacies that we leave behind, whether they are technology advancements, cultural contributions, or ethical precepts, by the narrative. At the same time as it encourages us to construct a legacy that is not limited by the constraints of time, it also encourages contemporary society to contemplate the continuation of human achievement.

7.4 Closing scenes with the protagonist sharing the truth with the world and the legacy of the Indus Valley Civilization

The story is getting closer and closer to its end, and the characters find themselves at a crossroads where they must choose between responsibility and revelation. The final scenes reveal a significant chapter, which is a point when the characters are required to reveal the truth to the rest of the world. Armed with the deciphered information of the ancient civilization's goal and the reasons behind its disappearance, the moments unfold in the final scenes. In this investigation, we delve into the emotional and intellectual climax that occurs when the legacy of the Indus Valley Civilization is revealed. This civilization left an indelible mark on the fabric of human history.

The Weight of knowledge: The final scenes begin with the characters struggling to come to terms with the knowledge that they are carrying with them. Not only does the old knowledge represent a historical curiosity, but it also represents a transformational power that has the capacity to influence modern understanding. This is because the ancient information has been decoded and understood. As the characters come face to face with the magnitude of the responsibility that has been placed upon them—to communicate a truth that is timeless—emotions are at an all-time high.

Within the narrative, the personal journeys of the protagonists are ingeniously woven together with the greater ramifications of the ancient knowledge. It is a tribute to the human capacity to bear the weight of history and to mold the future that this revelation becomes a burden for the human race.

Confronting Skepticism and Disbelief: As the characters make their insights public, the story delves into the complicated terrain of skepticism and disbelief. This occurs as the protagonists walk into the public realm. A mixture of curiosity, incredulity, and resistance is the response that the world gives because it is not used to rejecting the accepted historical narratives that it has been using. When confronted with a sea of doubters, skeptics, and those who are unwilling to embrace the paradigm-shifting truth, the characters find themselves in a difficult situation.

The depiction of society attitudes becomes a profound reflection on the difficulties that come with changing the existing quo.

The narrative encourages readers to contemplate the human propensity to cling to narratives that are familiar to them, as well as the bravery that is required to reject beliefs that have been held for a long time.

In the last scenes, the choice of the media through which the truth is communicated becomes an essential component. This is referred to as the medium of revelation. A dramatic public address, a finely produced historical display, or the publication of a ground-breaking scholarly paper might all be included in the tale. The protagonists, regardless of whether they are addressing a small group of people or standing in front of a large audience, make use of the media that they have chosen to communicate the breadth and impact of their discoveries.

Through the use of storytelling, visual representation, and the written word, the tale investigates the impact that these elements have in changing public opinion. The media functions as a vehicle through which the legacy of the old civilization is conveyed to a world that is eager to comprehend it.

Collaboration and Validation: In their efforts to disseminate the truth, the protagonists may look to the academic community for both collaboration and validation in their endeavors. Scenarios of collaboration with archaeologists, historians, and scientists who give their expertise to authenticate the veracity of the found knowledge are revealed throughout the narrative.

The representation of collaborative efforts places an emphasis on the interdisciplinary nature of historical inquiry and highlights the significance of peer review and validation in the process of discovering the truth. The story encourages readers to have an appreciation for the collaborative effort that is the process of solving historical mysteries.

Global Impact and Societal Transformation: As the truth is revealed, the story investigates the global impact that the revelations have had on society. Across the globe, societies are struggling to come to terms with the ramifications of a rewritten history, and the legacy of the ancient civilization extends beyond the confines of geographical bounds. In the final scenes, societal revolution is depicted, with the newly acquired information having an impact not only on academic circles but also on cultural, political, and social landscapes.

Through the course of the story, the narrative becomes a demonstration of the significant influence that historical discoveries can have on the formation of the collective consciousness of humanity. The publication encourages readers to contemplate the impact that history has had on the formation of present identities and narratives.

Ethical Considerations and Preservation: The closing scenes dig into the ethical considerations surrounding the preservation and sharing of the ancient wisdom. Conversations on responsible archaeology and cultural preservation are held between the characters, who are aware of the delicate balance that must be maintained between telling the truth and protecting the historical place.

Discussions about the ethical considerations involved in making sensitive information public, the potential impact on the archeological site, and the responsibilities that come with uncovering the past are woven throughout the narrative. It provides readers with the opportunity to reflect on the ethical implications of historical research as well as the delicate dance that takes place between the spread of information and the preservation of history.

The story shifts its focus to the enduring influence of the Indus Valley Civilization as the truth is revealed and the reactions of society are revealed. This occurs as the narrative approaches the seventh chapter. Scenes that illustrate the adoption of ancient cultural practices into modern living, the adaption of architectural designs in modern structures, or the incorporation of ancient knowledge into present schooling offer a striking image of the lasting impact that civilization has had for the world.

In the last scenes, there is a celebration of continuity, which is a recognition that the legacy of the past is not isolated to history books but is instead woven into the fabric of present existence. A reflection on the manner in which the lessons of history impact the present and contribute to the ongoing narrative of human civilization is something that the narrative encourages readers to consider.

Personal thoughts and Transformations: The last scenes provide glimpses into the personal thoughts and transformations that the protagonists have gone through throughout the course of the story. They struggle with the weight of their discoveries and the part they played in rewriting historical narratives. Having taken on the burden of uncovering the past, they are now wrestling with the weight of their discoveries.

An examination of the emotional toll and personal development that the protagonists go through is the focus of the tale, which transforms into a character study. Readers are encouraged to identify with the challenges of carrying the torch of historical truth and the transformational impact of connecting with the secrets of the past through the use of this book.

Future Possibilities and Unanswered Questions: Despite the fact that the concluding scenes bring conclusion to certain aspects of the story, they also leave room for future possibilities and questions that have not been resolved. Following the revelation of the truth, the characters may find themselves confronted with new queries, unexplored routes, and the possibility of further discovery.

An awareness that the uncovering of the past is an ongoing journey with no final destination is reflected in the story, which becomes a tribute to the ever-evolving character of historical investigation. It encourages readers to accept the mysteries that continue to exist as well as the possibility of further discoveries in the future.

As the story draws to a close, the heroes find themselves at a crossroads between the past and the present. They have just revealed the truth about the Indus Valley Civilization, and they are standing at the intersection of the two. The voyage, both emotionally and intellectually, becomes a reflection on the potential of historical discovery to transform perspectives, challenge preconceptions, and leave a legacy that will last for generations to come. A contemplation on the role of history in molding societies, promoting understanding, and contributing to the ongoing narrative of the human journey through time is invited by the narrative as the characters and readers alike struggle to come to terms with the repercussions of the truth that is shared. The concluding scenes serve not just as a conclusion but also as a gateway into the boundless opportunities that exist for historical research and the rich tapestry of stories that are just waiting to be discovered.